How to Acquire the Right Business

How to Acquire the Right Business

Right Business

John Psarouthakis and Lorraine Uhlaner

To order additional copies of this book, contact:
Xlibris Corporation
1-888-795-4274
www.Xlibris.com
Orders@Xlibris.com
51046

Contents

DEDICATION

To the daring entrepreneurs who have the imagination, intelligence and pragmatic sense to step out define what they want to buy, search, evaluate, negotiate, finance, develop an action plan and purchase the right business.

Acknowledgments

We like to express our appreciation to several individuals who provided us with their views in writing this book but are too numerous to mention all by name. However, our thanks do go especially to Kent Talcott, Donna Bacon, Jim Fahrner who provided helpful inputs, and Charlotte Daniels for her patient transliteration of the draft material.

PREFACE

This book reflects the firsthand, practical experience in the acquisition of businesses by the author John Psarouthakis. He has led the buying process for over forty acquisitions and has been a part of a team of a dozen others during his business career as an entrepreneur and business executive. Most of his experience comes from purchasing and selling businesses for two companies, J.P. Industries Inc. and JPE Inc. that he founded, managed, and eventually sold, as well as from the notes for the course on acquisitions he taught at the Ross School of Business of the University of Michigan as an adjunct professor of business.

Although Psarouthakis's experience draws heavily on the manufacture and distribution of durable goods sectors, many aspects of the process are the same, regardless of the industry.

Interviews conducted by coauthor Lorraine Hendrickson with entrepreneurs involved in acquisitions for the retailing, service, and construction sectors and other published information about the acquisitions process also influence the content of this book.

This book will systematically take you through the key steps in buying any company: *deciding* what you want to do, *finding* businesses for sale, *evaluating* business prospects, *negotiating* the deal, *financing* the deal, *closing* the acquisition, and *development of an action plan* prior to closing the deal and taking over the business (what to do once you own it).

This book will be useful to individuals who are contemplating the idea of buying and running a business, to those who plan to make numerous acquisitions, and to those business development executives whose goal is to make relevant acquisitions for meeting the growth goals and/or for the diversification strategy of the corporation.

We believe that the book will be of most help for deals of small- to medium-size range though the basic aspects of the process described here are applicable to any-size deal and though the details will differ significantly.

EVERY ACQUISITION HAS ITS OWN REQUIREMENTS AND PARTICULARITIES. THEREFORE, ALL AGREEMENTS AND DOCUMENTS SHOULD NOT BE MADE OR USED WITHOUT THE ADVICE OF LEGAL COUNSEL. THE AUTHORS ASSUME NO RESPONSIBILITY FOR THE USE OR MISUSE OF ANY OF THE CONTENT AND SAMPLE EXAMPLES CONTAINED IN THIS BOOK.

CHAPTER 1

INTRODUCTION: HOW TO ACQUIRE THE RIGHT BUSINESS

Buying a company is a demanding, complex process requiring a wide range of skills and abilities. If you understand this process thoroughly, then you are far more likely to make the right purchase decision. Whether you are buying the corner ice cream parlor or a $100-million business, following certain steps will enhance your chances of successfully operating a profitable venture once the deal is closed. This book should help you to visualize what really goes on in the making of a business deal.

Basis for the Book

Information for the book is drawn from several sources. The book heavily reflects the firsthand, practical experience in deal making by the author Dr. John Psarouthakis. He has led the buying process for about forty acquisitions and has been a part of a team of a dozen others during his business career as an entrepreneur and business executive. Most of his direct experience comes from purchasing and selling deals for his own two companies, J.P. Industries Inc. and JPE Inc.

In the 1980s, Psarouthakis founded and built J.P. Industries into a *Fortune 500* company by acquiring underperforming auto parts and plumbing products manufacturers, selling the company to a British conglomerate, T&N Plc in 1990. Next, he founded JPE Inc., which manufactured and distributed auto and truck parts for OEM and the aftermarket. Although Psarouthakis's experience draws heavily on the manufacture and distribution of durable goods sectors, many aspects of the process are the same, regardless of the industry. Interviews conducted by coauthor Lorraine Hendrickson with entrepreneurs involved in acquisitions for the retailing, service, and construction sectors and other published information about the acquisitions process also influence the content of this book.

The Buying Infrastructure

It is estimated by various sources that tens of thousands of businesses change ownership every year. For an updated estimate of this high-volume activity, contact the *International Business Brokers Association*. To support the very high number of transactions, a rather broad and complex infrastructure exists for finding and promoting deals. Few businesses up for sale are advertised in published sources. Relying upon this infrastructure is likely to provide you with a larger number of high-quality leads to choose from and with less effort than trying to find them on your own.

To be taken seriously within the business-investment community, you typically must demonstrate an understanding of the deal-making process, even if you hire consultants to assist you in the search.

The Importance of Careful Planning

A carefully planned and executed search process is likely to improve your odds of finding a company with which you can be successful. Too often, people rush into deals only to find out later that they did not purchase what they had expected. They suffer negative business consequences, such as lower than anticipated profits and sales. The alternative, careful planning may cost more initially and require more effort but is likely to lead to better business results in the long run.

Various studies have found that as high as 60% of acquisitions made fail to meet the acquisition-performance goals, ROI, ROE, etc., that were set at the closing and which influenced significantly the price paid. Just 25% met or exceeded those goals; the remaining 15% were indeterminate. There is one overriding reason for this high rate of failure and that is overpaying for the acquired company. Overpayment is a result of (1) an overoptimistic expectation of the market, (2) a higher-than-realistic estimate of internal improvements/developments, and (3) allowing oneself to enter a bidding war with the seller. In order to avoid as much as possible the above, this book presents a process based on many years of experience that resulted in the acquisition of over fifty deals and equivalently the sale of such acquired companies.

Successful Acquisition Process—16 Steps

One enters into a rather specific process when one decides to acquire a business and particularly the "right" business. You must manage and control the process if the result is to have a good chance to be the desired one. The acquisitions process involves several distinct steps and substeps that need to be attended to with extreme care and dealt with expertly and skillfully. These steps are the following:

1. Know what you want to acquire.
2. Set up criteria to guide you on what you want to buy.
3. Set up a plan on how you will proceed.
4. Identify/build a team that will work, do, and manage the process with you.
5. Develop a network of credible sources for acquisition candidates.
6. Screen carefully and thoroughly the candidates using the criteria set.
7. Conduct an effective preliminary evaluation/due diligence before you spend a great deal of time and money.
8. Negotiations really begin at the first meeting with the owner or his/her representatives. Preliminary agreements take place then and should be included in a letter of intent.
9. Involve your attorney early in the process and also with the letter of intent.

10. Conduct a thorough evaluation/due diligence. Look for surprises, but do not panic.
11. Develop a detailed action plan and complete it before you close the deal.
12. Review the value and price of the business with your colleagues.
13. Negotiate the purchase agreement with the full participation of your attorney.
14. Close the deal.
15. Begin implementation of the action plan immediately.
16. Last, but most important, meet as many people of the company as possible during the acquisition process. Do not wait to meet them after you close the deal.

Overview of the Buying Process

This book will systematically take you through the key steps in buying any company: deciding what you want to do finding businesses for sale evaluating business prospects negotiating the deal financing the deal closing the deal, and development of an action plan prior to taking over the business and prior to closing the deal (what to do once you own it)

Screening and the Buying Process

Figure 1.1 presents a simple representation of the buying process. Imagine several hundred leads entering the funnel on the far left. These are generated by the broker network that you build for your search. As the lead pool progresses through a succession of filters in the funnel, most leads are screened out by the initial filter, based on your initial criteria for size, type of industry, and profitability level. You may sign confidentiality agreements for as many as fifty companies over the course of your search. However, once you get more detailed information, you may quickly eliminate about half of this smaller group. The company might be in the wrong location, you may not be interested in the product line, or some other fact may be sent to you with initial materials that help you to rule that company out as a possible acquisition candidate. For any that still interest you, you might make an appointment to meet with the seller for further consideration. The latter procedure is typical when an investment banker is managing the deal for the seller.

Over the course of perhaps a year or two, you may further scrutinize several dozen candidates with a preliminary due diligence. In preliminary due diligence, you visit the company and obtain additional materials that help you weed out less acceptable candidates, even at this stage. For those that continue to interest you, you sign a letter of intent, which, though nonbinding, is an initial proposal to purchase the company that you present to the seller. At that point, you proceed through formal due diligence, and typically, though not always, through to a closing of the deal.

At any point in the screening process, you may come across information that leads you to a decision to abandon the negotiations for that company. For this reason, you must keep your lead flow active. That is, you continue to contact brokers and others in your network and continue to review leads. This helps to prevent the psychology of feeling compelled to go through with a "bad" deal just because you have progressed this far or spent so much time with it. Relative to the costs of owning and operating a company riddled with problems, you are still better off starting over than going through with a deal that is wrong for you.

If you have done your homework thoroughly at each step, you are less likely to reach an impasse in the later stages of negotiations, but it may happen. You may uncover a costly pollution problem, or the seller may reveal a serious product liability problem that had been hidden up to that point. Although this representation makes it appear that all the leads pass through at the same time, this is not the case. New leads continually enter the "funnel" while others drop out. Over the course of a year or two, you may screen as many as 200-300 leads. Most will drop out early on, in the screening process, some perhaps later at the preliminary or even the formal due diligence stage. A few may even get close to closing and still drop out. Eventually, if you are patient, you will find a suitable company for your needs.

Patience: Key to a Successful Search

Perhaps the most difficult part is finding the right business that you want and having the patience to wait it out until you find the right company. The other steps, such as evaluation, financing, pricing, and closing are straightforward. We cannot overemphasize the danger of rushing prematurely to purchase a company before you have carefully followed all the steps in the process. The process is designed to identify the company that you are likely to have the greatest likelihood of operating profitably and successfully. If you have several leads going at once, you are less apt to rush yourself into the wrong deal or even prematurely into the formal due diligence process, which is the most costly aspect of the deal making, prior to closing the deal. As you run out of money to investigate companies, you will be more likely to jump at the wrong opportunity. A good way to avoid this is to carry out several inexpensive screening steps before getting your accountant and attorney involved in formal due diligence.

The importance of careful screening cannot be overemphasized and indeed is borne out by other research. In their review of acquisitions made by twenty different companies, Philippe Haspeslagh of INSEAD (a French business school) and David Jemison of the University of Texas concluded that inadequate attention to screening was a *key* reason for poor performance of acquired firms. Although they looked at a sample of large companies, it would seem logical that this would hold true even more for the first-time buyer.

The Importance of Keeping the Leads Flowing

The importance of keeping a flow of leads going until you have closed the deal is illustrated from our own direct experience. With one company, we had several sessions of negotiating. We liked the company when we looked at it. But time moved on. Other deals were flowing into the funnel. The seller, in this case, became more and more demanding, which is his right, of course. But in the meantime, other companies entered the picture that appeared more attractive to us. We decided not to buy the company after all. Perhaps if we had not had those alternatives, we would have been more apt to go ahead with the deal, even though it would not have been a good one for us. The lesson here is a simple one: Even while you are negotiating a deal until you have closed the deal, you should keep your flow of leads coming in. It gives you another opportunity to ask yourself, "is this the deal I really should go through with?" It helps you from rushing into the deal and overpaying. This becomes especially true, late in the negotiations process. You may have already spent a fair amount of time and money on formal due diligence. But beware of escalating commitment. Don't ever feel locked in or hooked on the deal. Just keep looking. By having several "irons in the fire," you are less likely to get emotionally fixated on any one company.

When you start hiring lawyers and accountants to help with the due diligence, the costs can quickly escalate and thus your emotional commitment to the deal. This brings up another general guideline to keep in mind. Don't bring in the heavy-cost items until you are pretty sure you will succeed with that deal. At any point in the process, when you encounter a serious problem, don't proceed with any other activity until this is straightened out.

A very common problem that crops up in this category is environmental pollution. It's not a matter of dishonesty. Many well-meaning owners are not even aware of problems that have been created in their own companies. In one lead we pursued, a company had removed some storage tanks years before and built a slab basement factory floor over their previous location. Unfortunately, the tanks had leaked into the groundwater prior to their removal. What initially started as a routine check turned into an extensive and more expensive investigation. Eventually, it was determined that although serious, the pollution problem was fairly well contained and other aspects of the due diligence process were continued. In another case, we convinced the seller to set up a "cleanup" fund of $5 million dollars, which turned out to be more than adequate to cover the eventual cleanup costs.

The Buying Process as a Problem-Solving Process

Another effective way to understand the buying process is to view it as a problem-solving process. As questions or problems emerge, you try

---

19

to solve them with the seller. Some deals may encounter unresolvable problems at which point you may have to drop the deal altogether. Locating the right business is expensive and time-consuming. You want to avoid dropping a lead, especially in the late stages, just because a minor difference in price or point of view between buyer and seller creates an impasse, and yet this often takes place. Although you should heed the advice to avoid rushing into a deal, don't drop a deal either just because of some detail. Build rapport with the seller. Negotiating skill and experience help to reduce the risk of losing out on a deal because of some minor difficulty.

Organization of the Book

This book is designed to cover the buying process in detail from the moment you decide that you would like to buy a company to the day you take over. This section describes the organization of the book and what is covered in each chapter.

Deciding What You Want to Do

Before actually beginning to shop for a company, you must establish a clear focus. What are your personal goals for buying the business? You need to consider your own experience first. *Chapter 2: Who Buys Companies and Why?* presents information you might consider in evaluating your own readiness for taking on business ownership, including your motives and preparation for business.

Once you have made the decision to buy a company and before beginning the actual search, you also need to decide on the type of business you are looking for. You must also establish broad criteria for your search and begin development of a business plan.

Chapter 3: Criteria and the Acquisition Plan presents guidelines for these broad criteria. Initial criteria should fit the type of information you are likely to obtain. Typically, you are limited to very general information at the beginning: size, profitability of the business, and the industry sector. Once you sign a confidentiality agreement for a particular business lead, you are likely to have access to more detailed information about company performance, product line, exact location, and other information. As you progress through negotiations, from the signing of a confidentiality agreement to the letter of interest, letter of intent, purchase agreement and closing, your screening criteria become more detailed and your investigation more in-depth as you continue to obtain new information about the deal.

You also need to consider, early on, what you want to do with the business: fix it up and sell it, buy and keep it a long time, or build a group of businesses. This is an important decision because it affects the type of business you seek and the investors and financing you are likely to attract.

Chapter 4: Building Credibility for Business Ownership describes the credibility issue. Establishing credibility within the business-investment community is an essential step in finding the right business. Credibility is also essential to obtain financing for the deal, to attract investors, and to attract competent consultants and employees to help you before and after you buy your firm. Without it, you are not likely to succeed.

Chapter 5: Building the Acquisition Team You are not likely to find the right business all by yourself. If you plan to be successful, early on, you will need to develop an acquisition team. This chapter will familiarize you with the type of team members you will need at different points in the process and what to look for when hiring team members, whether as consultants or as employees.

Finding Businesses for Sale

Finding the right business is a time-consuming process. Your success in locating the right business depends upon your credibility in the business-investment community and your patience to develop and cast a wide net to establish the flow of business leads.

Chapter 6: Casting the Net for Business Leads explains how you find leads. It describes the sources for leads as well as a recommended approach for managing your business-deal lead flow over time. Expect to take a year or even two years before finding the right company. Rushing into the wrong deal is one of the most common mistakes buyers make. Stick to your original criteria and goals, and you will eventually find the right company. It is not unusual to sift through several hundred leads before finding the right company.

Evaluating the Business Acquisitions Prospects

Chapter 7: Narrowing Your Search: Matching Broad Criteria of Your Initial Business Plan describes the first few steps of this process in greater detail, whether you are dealing with a private broker or investment banker. Chapter 8 will introduce you to important documents at this step, including the confidentiality agreement and letter of interest, needed to obtain more detailed information about those companies you are exploring.

Chapter 8: The Evaluation Process: An Overview explains how evaluation of the acquisition prospect is an ongoing process that begins the moment you obtain a lead from a broker. The overview of this process is presented in this chapter.

Chapter 9: Preliminary Due Diligence describes the next step in the evaluation process. Once you have signed a confidentiality agreement and have access to more information about the company, you are in the position to filter out companies that might have looked attractive but upon closer inspection do not meet your criteria. Chapter 9 describes the types of information you are likely to obtain at this stage and what you want to review. If you started with several hundred leads, you may only complete a preliminary due diligence on several dozen. It is important to realize that you have still not invested much money on this stage in reviewing each acquisition candidate. Primarily, you have spent your own time to review materials, and typically, to visit the company up for sale to meet with the owner and key managers.

Once you have completed a preliminary due diligence, you may decide not to pursue a company. If you are still interested and before you actually begin to invest significant amounts of funds in conducting detailed investigations, obtaining expert opinions and efforts from accountants, consultants, lawyers, or other specialists (such as environmental protection), it would be wise to negotiate with the assistance of a skilled lawyer and to sign a letter of intent. This letter protects both the buyer and seller. During a designated period, the seller agrees not to sell to anyone else. In turn, the buyer may have to agree to pay a penalty if he or she decides with no reason not to complete the deal. However, it is unwise to progress and spend thousands of dollars without some guarantee of this sort from the seller.

Chapter 10: Letter of Intent and Formal Due Diligence provides a detailed account of the letter of intent and the formal due diligence process, the final leg in the evaluation process.

You actually begin valuing and pricing a company from the very moment you obtain initial information about the company. If you are required to sign a letter of interest, you may be asked early in the negotiations process to suggest a price that you might be interested in paying. However, this price is nonbinding, and pricing and valuing are continually modified as you learn more about the company, up until closing.

Chapter 11: Valuing and Pricing the Company provides an introduction to this very important component of business evaluation that helps you to determine what the company worth is and what price to offer the seller for his or her company. It also discusses some aspects of the process of valuing and pricing that takes place throughout negotiations.

Negotiating the Deal

Negotiations actually begin with the very first contacts that you make with the seller and/or his or her broker. The negotiations process and general tips in the negotiation process are both described in *Chapter 12: Negotiating the Deal.*

Financing the Deal

Chapter 13: Financing the Acquisition describes different sources of capital and other issues you need to consider when financing the acquisition.

The Action Business Plan

As you approach closing, you must anticipate many of the issues that you will need to address once you take over—options that you want to take as you are about to own and manage the business. It is wise to develop a detailed action business plan that is to be implemented on the day of the takeover. Some of your initial business plan may be useful, but you are advised to prepare a more detailed document. *Chapter 14: Preparing an Acquisition Action Plan* discusses this very important aspect of the acquisition process.

Closing the Deal

Once you have finally arranged for financing and negotiating a price with the seller, and you are satisfied that you have thoroughly evaluated the prospective company, you are ready to close the deal. *Chapter 15: Closing the Deal* describes key issues and concerns to be wary of at this stage to assure a smooth closing and transition. It also describes the purchase agreement, the legal document that binds seller and buyer in the deal. *Chapter 16: After the Deal is Closed: Smoothing the Transition to New Ownership* deals with the activities that should take place immediately after closing the deal at which time you own the business.

Recommended Readings

1. F. Meeks and N. Rotenier "Am I Going to Mind Sweeping the Floors?", *Forbes*, Vol. 152, issue 11, November 8, 1993, pp.142-148.

2. P. C. Haspeslagh and D. Jemison, *Managing Acquisitions: Creating value through corporate renewal* (New York: Free Press, 1991).

Figure 1.1 Anatomy of the Buying Process

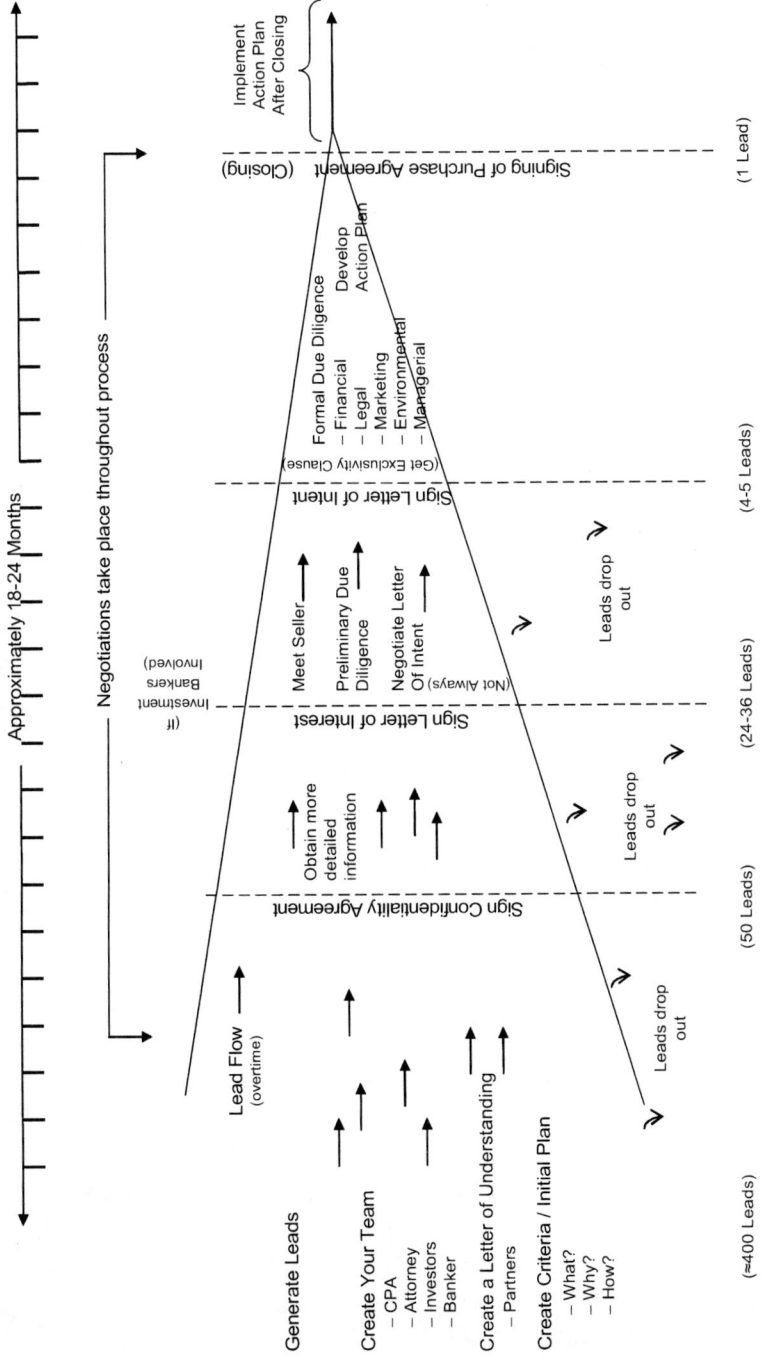

Approximately 18-24 Months

Negotiations take place throughout process

Implement
Action Plan
After Closing

Signing of Purchase Agreement (Closing)   (1 Lead)

Formal Due Diligence
– Financial
– Legal
– Marketing
– Environmental
– Managerial

Develop
Action Plan

Sign Letter of Intent   (4-5 Leads)
(Get Exclusivity Clause)

Meet Seller

Preliminary Due
Diligence

Negotiate Letter
Of Intent

Leads drop
out

(If
Investment
Bankers
Involved)

(Not Always)

Sign Letter of Interest   (24-36 Leads)

Obtain more
detailed
information

Leads drop
out

Sign Confidentiality Agreement   (50 Leads)

Lead Flow
(overtime)

Generate Leads

Create Your Team
– CPA
– Attorney
– Investors
– Banker

Create a Letter of Understanding
– Partners

Create Criteria / Initial Plan
– What?
– Why?
– How?

Leads drop
out

(≈400 Leads)

CHAPTER 2

WHO BUYS COMPANIES AND WHY

If you are buying a business for the first time, you will find that buying a business is a unique experience that requires extensive knowledge and skills in a broad spectrum of areas—legal, accounting, banking, financing, the understanding of government regulations, especially in areas of environment, safety, and employee relations. You must learn how to obtain and screen leads, how to evaluate and price prospective companies, and how to conduct due diligence. But even highly experienced entrepreneurs who have completed dozens of deals still rely upon professional expertise for certain phases of the process. Thus expect that even after you learn more about the deal-making process, you will still need to hire consultants to assist you in making a successful purchase.

Buying a company is very demanding because it is an intellectual, pragmatic, and emotional process all in one. It is an *intellectual* process because to be successful, you have to think it out. It is a *pragmatic* process because you have to be realistic about the company you are looking to buy, whether it is worth buying, what its real value is, and what it should be priced at. And buying a company, finally, is an *emotional* process. Throughout negotiations, beginning with first contact with the seller and continuing through to the closing of the sale, you experience tremendous highs and lows. You must be able to handle both extremes of emotion. You must handle the highs, so as not to reveal your enthusiasm to the seller, and after the lows, to be able to come back and find a solution to the problem that might otherwise kill the deal. The emotional component holds true even after many deals, but you do learn to control those emotions with practice.

Reasons for Buying Your Own Business

Some of the reasons for buying your own business are similar to those of any entrepreneur: control of your own destiny, the personal challenge, making money, and the satisfaction of building and running something on your own.

In addition, some individuals may find buying an established business more appealing than starting from scratch. These issues are explored in the following section.

Buying a Company Holds Less Risk Than Starting from Scratch

Three avenues are open to the budding entrepreneur: starting from scratch, buying a franchise, or buying another established business. Although most books on entrepreneurship devote a chapter, at best, to buying a company, it is becoming an increasingly popular avenue to business ownership.

Some evidence suggests that buying a business is less risky than starting from scratch. According to business brokers, four out of five small businesses that change hands are still in business five years later. By contrast, the Small Business Administration claims that two in five individuals survive for six years.[1] And although franchising is a popular direction, recent reports suggest it may actually be more risky than starting from scratch.[2]

Other research that compares start-up ventures within larger organizations to acquisition of firms points to another important reason

---

[1] F. Meeks and N. Rotinier, "Am I going to mind sweeping the floors?", *Forbes*, Vol. 152, Issue 11, Nov. 8, 1993, pp.142-148.

[2] April or May, 1995 Inc. Magazine or Fortune Magazine. [NOTE: Needs to go on page 27 and locate reference]

for buying a company. Ralph Biggadike of the University of Virginia found that on average it takes eight years for a new venture to reach profitability. It takes ten to twelve years before the average venture equals that of a mature business. Cash flow typically remains negative for the first eight years. By contrast, it is possible for a company to purchase a market leader in a strong cash position overnight.[3] In another study, Edwin Mansfield of the University of Pennsylvania concluded that only between 12% and 20% of research and development based new ventures actually succeed in earning an economic profit at all.[4]

Of course, the individual buying the smaller company may have a different experience base, but the general pattern remains. Most new ventures take years to pay off. With careful screening, you are likely to obtain far more rapid return on your investment via acquisition of an existing company *if* you are careful to purchase the right company in the first place.

Timing: When Should You Start?

Because of the lack of existing research on the topic, most of what we assume to be true about entrepreneurs who buy businesses is based on the larger sample of all entrepreneurs who start and own their own businesses and based on our own observation. Adults, young and old, may buy and start a business, but some of the key issues will be different for those in different age brackets. Figure 2.1 summarizes some of the key issues typically faced by adults at different stages in adulthood that Daniel J. Levinson and colleagues published in *The Seasons of a Man's Life.*[5] A typical adult acquires relevant business

---

[3] E. R. Biggadike, *Corporate Diversification: Entry, Strategy and Performance* (Cambridge, Mass: Division of Research, Harvard Business School, 1983).

[4] E. Mansfield, "How Economists See R&D," *Harvard Business Review* (November-December, 1981) pp.98-106.

[5] D. J. Levinson, et al *The Seasons of a Man's Life*, (New York: Alfred A. Knopf, 1978), as cited in J. A.Timmons and S. Spinelli, *New Venture Creation*, 7th edition (Boston, MA: McGraw-Hill, 2007).

---

and work experience beginning in his or her early to mid-20s. Thus an adult of about thirty-five years of age can be expected to have about 10-15 years of meaningful work experience. This is the average age for males starting their first venture with the average age of females being slightly higher, at about thirty-eight.[6] Recent research evidence suggests that business education and experience in general managerial positions is associated with a greater likelihood of success as an entrepreneur.[7]

The framework summarized in Figure 2.1 also assumes that as we get older, we typically take on responsibilities such as a house mortgage, spouse, or children that may reduce our perceived ability to take risks or change jobs. And as we age further, even when some of those responsibilities lessen, radical change in our lifestyles becomes more difficult.

Age is also likely to impact the credibility that the would-be entrepreneur is likely to have and the related ability to obtain financing from the bank. It usually takes several years for most adults to accumulate savings, contacts, and access to financing unless inherited from a parent or other family member.

Although these are factors to consider, however, none is probably as important in determining the appropriateness of your own decision to buy a company as is your strong desire to be the owner of a company. Also we would like to add that in our view and our own experience, the above become more relevant in the manufacturing business. As we all know, in the high-tech field and particularly in the computer and internet-related businesses, a number of individuals have succeeded greatly at a rather young age.

---

[6]   R. Hisrich and M. Peters, *Entrepreneurship: Starting, Developing and Managing a New Enterprise*, 3rd edition, (Chicago: Irwin, 1995) p.44.

[7]   G.N. Chandler, and E. Jansen, "The Founder's Self-Assessed Competence and Venture Performance," *Journal of Business Venturing*, Vol. 7, May, 1992, pp. 223-236

The Young Company Buyer

The youngest group of company purchasers, typically, those in their twenties, are most likely to encounter problems of credibility because they simply haven't had the time to develop the expertise in business. They are also less likely to have adequate monetary resources to finance their acquisition. And they are likely to have a less effective network for obtaining leads, for obtaining funds, and for obtaining professional assistance needed to assist in the buying process and later to manage the business.

On the other hand, the young person is more likely to feel comfortable taking risks. He or she often has fewer family obligations. The younger individual is likely to have a higher energy level and perhaps a higher level of need to succeed. However, it is important to keep in mind that greater willingness to take risks does not necessarily mean a greater probability of success. However, when the right deal comes along, the younger person may be less likely to hesitate and let the deal get away.

Key to preparation for the younger buyer is credibility and financing. Although people generally view a younger person as having less experience and therefore less credibility, there are ways to offset this perception. And although, other things being equal, the banks might be reluctant to lend to an inexperienced individual, a carefully developed business plan, a sound group of advisors and credible investors can go a long way toward changing a banker's mind. The topic of credibility will be revisited in greater depth in chapter 3.

The More Mature Company Buyer

The more mature company buyer (anywhere between 40 and 60, depending upon years of actual work experience), that individual with 15-20 years of experience in business or a particular industry, is likely to have more credibility with both the broker and banking communities, access to greater monetary resources, and a more well-developed network to draw upon for business leads, investments, and professional assistance. The more senior company buyer may also be more focused, having had more years of experience learning about the types of work and industries he is interested in. But he or she is also, at least psychologically speaking, running out of time. Although people are certainly keeping fit and continuing to work longer than before, there is also the likelihood that the fifty-year-old has fewer years before retirement than does the twenty-year-old. This might affect the interest of certain investors, but more importantly, it may limit the number of years available to the prospective buyer to make a firm profitable.

The Optimum Point of Departure

There is no one perfect time to buy a business. However, the prospective buyer in midcareer (perhaps 35-40 years of age) may have the ideal balance of work experience, credibility, networking, and access to financing to step out and begin to buy existing businesses. The married individual will have to pay careful attention to a personal family plan to prepare himself or herself and his or her family for possible financial and nonfinancial sacrifices for a period before and even after the business is purchased. This is not to say that someone younger or older cannot do very well. But the youngest individuals will have to address credibility issues much more vigorously. And more senior individuals, generally speaking, may have to overcome greater inertia toward change although sometimes downsizing and restructuring within companies forces people in midcareer and late career to reconsider their career choices anyway.

The most important thing to keep in mind, regardless of your age, experience, and circumstances is your strong desire to go into business. Otherwise, the rest won't fall into line. You need tremendous motivation in order to generate the enthusiasm and to put the necessary time and work required into your business to assure its success.

You must articulate certain critical guiding rules. These rules must be specific, not general. They must reflect your vision, your experience, your and your team's abilities, and must follow them with discipline and open mind. In my case and the case of the teams I lead, the following is a set of rules that we adhere to:

1. Have the support of your family.
2. Organize yourself and your team.

31

3. Define your own investment ability, and do not exceed it.
4. Define what is the "right" business for you.
5. Line up financial support: investors, banks.
6. Keep in mind that about 90% of those that try to buy a business do not complete a deal.
7. Do not get hooked (fall in love) by a business and its products/ services. Get hooked by its profitability.
8. Try to have a choice of two or three deals in the making to relieve the pressure of compromise.
9. Set the parameters that if you cannot meet, you will not make the deal. Just walk away from it.
10. Do not close the deal before completion of "your business action plan" that you intend to implement after closing.
11. Be at the purchased business in person immediately after closing and talk to the employees about yourself and your interest in the company

Chapter Summary

Buying a company is by far one of the most complex purchase activities most individuals ever undertake. A far broader array of skills and knowledge is required than for any other purchase, certainly much more so than purchasing a house or an automobile. And although an infrastructure exists, the prospective buyer is expected to be familiar with many of the rules of the game before undertaking such a venture, or he or she won't be taken seriously. Fair or not, age provides a rough yardstick by which many prospective buyers are initially measured by the broker and banking community. Younger buyers must overcome issues of credibility. Senior buyers must overcome the concern that they lack the energy and/or are too close to retirement to take the project seriously and must overcome their own hesitancy to start over with a new company. In spite of these obstacles, adults in a very wide range of ages successfully purchase and run their own companies. Strong drive or desire, among all the personal characteristics, is perhaps the single, most important ingredient in assuring their success.

Figure 2.1: Age and characteristics bearing on new venture start-ups

	Characteristic	20s	30s	40s	50s
1	Relevant Business Experience	Low	Moderate to high	Higher	Highest
2	Management Skills and Know-How	Low to moderate	Moderate to high	High	High
3	Entrepreneurial Goals and Commitment	Varies widely	Focused high	High	High
4	Drive and Energy	Highest	High	Moderate	Lowest
5	Risk-taking	Highest	Moderate to high	Moderate	Lowest
6	Credibility	Lowest	Moderate	High	High
7	Network	Lowest	Moderate	High	Highest
8	Access to Financial Resources	Lowest	Low to moderate	Moderate	Highest

Adapted from Daniel J. Levinson, et al *The Seasons of a Man's Life*, (New York: Alfred A. Knopf, 1978, and Jeffrey Timmons, *New Venture Creation*, Burr Ridge, Illinois: Irwin, 1994)

CHAPTER 3

CRITERIA AND THE
ACQUISITION PLAN

This chapter will assist you in clarifying the business decisions that you should make even before you identify the company you plan to buy. In particular, before launching into your new business venture, you should consider three important questions:

Why do you want to buy a company?

What type of company do you want to buy?

How are you going to go about buying the company?

The answers to these questions form the basis of the initial plan you need to take to prospective investors and bankers. You will screen and locate appropriate business leads more efficiently if you start with an initial plan. You will also generate greater interest by bankers and prospective investors in your venture. We recommend that you need to address the issues outlined in this chapter *before* you begin your search. The initial plan should not be confused with the action plan that you will need to develop once you identify the *particular* enterprise that you plan to purchase.

Clarify Your Goals for Owning a Business

Before you decide upon the type of company you want to buy, you need to clarify not only for yourself but also prospective lenders, investors, and sellers, why you are buying a company.

The issues examined in this section affect the way in which others view the seriousness of your purpose and whether they are interested in being a party to the project. For instance, do you plan to buy just one company or several? Will you run the company by yourself or get others to help? Do you plan to resell the business once you have improved its value, or do you plan to keep it for a long time? These decisions will in turn affect the size of company you seek, the level of investor interest, and the types of people you will need to help run your company. In particular, you need to answer the following types of questions for yourself before you begin to gather and screen leads:

1. *Do you want to run the business yourself, or do you want others to help you?* Is this a purchase you basically are making to provide yourself with self-employment as an alternative to working for someone else, or do you plan to have other highly skilled people in your management team?

2. *How long do you plan to keep the business?* That is, do you view this as a short-term or a long-term investment?

3. *Do you plan to buy other businesses?* Many buyers view the business purchase as a once-in-a-lifetime career move. Others may view this first purchase as a stepping-stone toward building a much larger business empire.

4. *If you're buying additional companies, do you plan to buy related or unrelated companies?* Until the 1980s, the unrelated conglomerate was looked upon favorably by investors. However, the rapid growth in global competition in an ever-widening number of industries makes it much harder for companies to be successful in diverse areas. The related conglomerate has

become an increasingly popular model for acquisition-oriented companies.

Who Will Run the Business

Many people buy a business to provide themselves with employment, first and foremost. This is certainly an acceptable objective, but if this is your intent, then you need to be careful to seek the size and type of company that you are prepared to manage on your own. Many first-time entrepreneurs, whether entering by way of start-up or purchase of an existing business, are shocked to learn of the complexities of operating even a relatively small company. A sole proprietorship with perhaps one or two part-time people is a completely different operation to manage than one with even a few dozen employees, with the complexity of operating the business rising almost exponentially with the increase in employment size. A company of one hundred, not to mention a few thousand employees, can be daunting to the president who has successfully managed a company of twenty or twenty-five employees.

If you plan to start with an experienced management team, especially one that includes those who have managed similar businesses in the past, then it is realistic for you to consider a wider range of options, including larger companies or those in more highly competitive industries. If your company must support this team full-time from the outset, it may be necessary to seek a company large enough to support this overhead as well.

How Long You Plan to Keep the Business

You should also consider whether you plan to keep your company over the long-term, which we will refer to as the *keeper* or if you plan to improve its value with the eye toward resale in the short term, which we will refer to as the *fixer-upper*.

The Keeper

Many business owners make perhaps only one or two purchases in their career, with the idea that they will buy the company with the intention of holding on to it for quite an extended period. This decision will dictate to some extent the type of company you look for. If you are primarily purchasing the company as a lifestyle change, to become your own boss, then you need to consider very seriously the importance of selecting a company that already performs fairly well, especially if the business is to be your primary means of support. You need to be realistic about the amount of time it might take for an underperforming business to be in the position of paying you well. Many skillfully led turnarounds may take a year or two or even longer although the smaller the company, the more quickly you might be able to turn it around.

The Fixer-Upper

Some buyers look for *fixer-uppers* to borrow a term from the real-estate business. They are more likely to seek an underperforming business with the interest of turning it around, thereby dramatically improving its value and reselling it. This type of strategy works well if you have relevant experience within the industry that the company is in. Many small, family-run businesses establish a favorable market niche but lack the business management skills in-house to track and control costs, to market effectively, or to introduce more efficient production and management techniques, for instance. They are often started by individuals lacking a formal business education and an understanding of the basic techniques taught in business schools. But at the same time, you should be cautioned against assuming that the introduction of such techniques alone will turn a company around. Experience in a particular industry is vital also to assure that you make the appropriate strategic decisions over time.

J.P. Industries pursued this strategy, looked for underperforming companies that, nevertheless, manufactured products with a solid reputation in the automobile industry. The company was founded with an experienced management team. Two key members of the team, including the CEO, came equipped with a mechanical engineering background and extensive manufacturing experience. This education and experience paid rich dividends. Improvements in earnings for most of the acquired firms showed up in less than a year, and the entire group was sold for a substantial profit to initial investors, about ten years after the start-up.

Key to J.P. Industries' success was the selection of businesses, though underperforming, that had a strong product reputation and revenue stream. We do not recommend purchasing a company with a poor product reputation. Turnaround in such cases is far more time-consuming and less certain than in situations where the product is doing well but the assets and expenses are managed poorly.

How Many Businesses You Plan to Buy

Investors and banks will also want to know whether your plans involve the intent to buy just one company or to buy several. You may be more likely to obtain interest in a project that aims to acquire a family of companies than a single company. On the other hand, such a project probably requires a much larger investment at the outset. It also requires a larger, more skilled management team.

At J.P. Industries Inc. or JPE Inc., banks would not have provided the multimillion-dollar credit line just to purchase one medium-sized company. They extended credit based upon the credibility of management on building a multiple business group successfully. In sum, if banks and investors know your objectives and strategy, they may view your situation more favorably.

If Buying Additional Companies, Do You Plan to Buy Related or Unrelated Companies?

If your ambition is to build a collection of companies into a larger corporation, then you have additional issues to consider. Do you plan to purchase several related companies and operate them together as a group? If you buy companies that are related, you have to understand the possible synergistic relations that may occur between the companies. This will tell you what types of people you need to have around you and what value you can generate due to synergies.

Another alternative is to assemble a group of unrelated companies into a portfolio, with the idea of improving their value for a while and then selling them. It is beyond the scope of this book to go into detail about portfolio acquisitions, but once again, these goals will impact other decisions that you make.

What Type of Company You Plan to Buy

Although many books list a rather long list of candidates, the truth is that very few leads come in detailed books. Most will likely come from small brokers, who generally have very limited information at the earliest stages. But you shouldn't ignore these candidates. The best way to handle them is to develop some rules of thumb about the criteria you will select.

Though you are likely to develop more detailed lists of criteria eventually, the three pieces of information you are apt to obtain from most brokers early on in the negotiations relate to industry, company size, and profitability. You will eventually need to consider many other issues, but practically speaking, at the start, you are not likely to get much more information than this until you sign a confidentiality agreement with the broker. Thus before you approach different sources for leads, you should clarify three issues in your mind:

1. What industry are you interested in?
2. How large a company do you want to purchase and manage?
3. How profitable does the company need to be?

The answers to these questions help you to narrow your pool of prospects from several hundred to several dozen over a period. Without clarifying these issues in your mind up-front, you might waste your time looking into companies that are not realistic for you to pursue.

The Type of Industry You Plan to Buy

Depending upon your background, you might already know the type of business you are interested in looking into. Perhaps you would like to buy a business in an industry that you are already involved with now. Or perhaps you are confident that a particular industry is likely to do well. Be careful to research the industry you are thinking of entering. What is the total size of the market, and is it growing or declining? Is there a particular niche within this industry that is doing particularly well? Be wary of jumping into an industry that you know little about. Try to find out as much as you can before making a final determination.

Which Size of Company You Plan to Buy

The size of company you buy will determine the amount of capital you will need to raise and the complexity of the task of managing the company once you own it. Think carefully about the size of company you are comfortable managing and/or the people to assist in its management. Operating a company with only a few employees is far less complex than a company with a hundred, not to mention a thousand employees. If you have not managed large groups of people in the past, you might want to consider very carefully before buying a larger firm.

Profitability of the Company You Plan to Buy

A company that is already generating a stable profit and cash flow is far easier to manage than one that is operating in the red. The companies in the latter category may be cheaper to obtain but may never generate a profit for you. If you have experience turning around companies and understand the cost structure of your industry and its marketing better than the present owners appear to, then buying an underperforming company can prove quite lucrative. That was indeed the strategy at J.P. Industries. On the other hand, especially when the economy is robust, it may be difficult to find a good acquisition candidate that is struggling and there may be more fundamental reasons that a company is doing poorly that are not easily remedied. Again, this comes back to your own experience in business and what you are capable of doing.

Your Plan for the Acquisition Process

Bankers, other lenders, and investors will also be interested to see your plan for the acquisition process itself, that is, how you plan to go about looking for your business. Once you have decided on the broad criteria of what you are looking for, you also need to determine how you are going to go about purchasing your company. Some of these issues include the following:

1. Where will you go for the money?
2. Who will help you in your search?
3. What personal arrangements will you need to make until you find and purchase the company?
4. How do you plan to find the right company?
5. What is your exit strategy?

Where You Will Go for the Money and What Will You Use It for

Investors and bankers will want to know what the money is for. Will you use it to build value in the company, pay down debt, etc.? They want to know how you are going to get your finances and manage your costs so that you get a higher output of results with a minimum of costs.

Even though you are not likely to get money from investors or a bank before actually locating the company you plan to buy, you cannot wait until that point to identify your funding sources. To gain credibility with prospective sellers and brokers, you need to work out in advance what type of financing arrangements you will use in case you do find a suitable choice. A bank will often give you a letter of understanding that will essentially say, "Yes, we will deal with you. Find a company and then we'll look at it and tell you whether we will give you a credit line (or loan or whatever)." This letter of understanding is important because it allows you to say to the seller that you have a personal relationship with John Doe at XYZ bank and that the seller can call to verify this relationship. Although it doesn't guarantee, of course, that you will get your loan or credit line, it does contribute to your credibility with the seller. When founding J.P. Industries, the CEO talked to a couple of investment banks and came to an understanding on a deal-by-deal basis. They gave permission for him to use their name in a brochure. Especially at the beginning, this was very helpful in establishing credibility.

Who Will Help You in Your Search

As soon as you respond to an initial contact from a broker or investment banker, you have initiated the negotiations process and may say and do things that will affect the outcome of the sale. It is wise therefore, even if you plan to do much of the work yourself in contacting brokers and prescreening leads, to seek input from your attorney and your accountant as soon as you begin to investigate particular prospects. You need to identify the professional people who will help you in your search *early* in the search process, probably even before you begin to accumulate and screen leads.

What Personal Arrangements You Need to Make

You should plan on your search, taking between one and two years if you want to avoid rushing into the wrong deal. Depending upon the size of company you are seeking, you may need to leave your present job if you want to be taken seriously in your endeavor. When Psarouthakis founded J.P. Industries, he left Masco Industries before embarking on his search. He developed a two-year financial plan together with the immediate family. It helps to be sure that everyone understands and will be supportive within your immediate family.

How You Plan to Find the Right Company

This part of your plan might be a simple one. For instance, you will use criteria to find the right company, plan to run advertisements in the *Wall Street Journal* to establish a network of finders and to begin relating to investment bankers. You will need to tell your backers you are going to manage your costs so that you can get the higher output of results with a minimum of costs. Chapter 6 will provide much more insight on the approaches to take in developing a lead flow of business prospects.

Your Exit Strategy

Finally, an initial plan needs to include your exit strategy. That is, how will investors be able to get their initial investment out of the business over time? Investors, in particular, will want to know whether you plan to go public or to sell the company. Or perhaps you plan to have a high level of dividend distribution of earnings. These issues are important to clarify right at the start because they might influence how you set up the legal structure of the company from a tax standpoint. For instance, with a regular corporation, you pay a double tax on dividends.

Of course, only a small subset of companies catch the public's interest in the market, so if that is your goal, you might consider certain types and sizes of companies. Both J.P. Industries and JPE Inc. were started with the idea that they would eventually be taken public.

Chapter Summary

An acquisition business plan needs to be developed before you begin your search to buy a company. The three overall categories of decisions need to be made are the following:

1. Why do you want to buy a company?
2. What type of company do you want to buy?
3. How are you going to go about buying the company?

In determining *why* you want to buy a company, you should ask yourself and develop answers for each of the following questions:

1. Do you want to run the business yourself, or do you want others to help you?

2. How long do you plan to keep the business?
3. Do you plan to buy other businesses over time?
4. If buying additional companies, do you plan to buy related or unrelated companies?

In determining *what* type of company you want to buy, you should ask yourself, at the outset the following questions:

1. What industry are you interested in?
2. How large a company do you want to purchase and manage?
3. How profitable does the company need to be?

And in developing a plan on *how* you plan to go about buying a company, resolving the following issues at the outset will affect the types of investors you will attract and potentially, how successful your search will be:

1. Where will you go for the money?
2. Who will help you in your search?
3. What personal arrangements will you need to make until you find and purchase the company?
4. How do you plan to find the right company?
5. What is your exit strategy? That is, how will investors be able to get their initial investment out of the business over time?

Clarifying these issues in your mind will advance your efforts at selecting the appropriate company.

CHAPTER 4

BUILDING CREDIBILITY FOR BUSINESS OWNERSHIP

Credibility is an intangible but essential ingredient in making a successful business deal. According to *Webster's Dictionary*, to be credible is to be "worthy of trust" or "believable." In business, it refers to the belief and perception of other people that you are able to do the things you propose to do. There is no scientific way to measure credibility or to assure that others believe in you. However, there are a number of tips outlined in this chapter to help increase the likelihood that others will take you seriously in a business deal.

General Qualities that Contribute to Credibility

Display of integrity, pragmatism, interpersonal skills, professionalism, and ability all contribute toward your credibility.

Integrity. Integrity refers to sincerity or honesty—that you mean what you say. A businessperson of integrity addresses the issues openly and directly. People feel that they can trust you and rely on your word. They do not fear that you will do something underhanded when their backs are turned.

Pragmatism. This is another quality that contributes toward a credible image. A pragmatic person understands the issues and is realistic.

Interpersonal Skills. Interpersonal skills can also contribute to your credibility. These skills involve your ability to communicate clearly with others and to be considerate of others.

Professionalism. How do you come across as professional? Be thorough in any detail you handle. Find out as much as you can about the companies and industries you plan to deal with so that you will appear knowledgeable. A person who approaches an issue with intelligence, analysis, and calmness is viewed as professional or objective in demeanor. Such demeanor generates respect and trust by others.

Knowledge of the Acquisition Process. Beyond your knowledge of the specific companies and industries, it is important that you convey knowledge of the acquisition process. You must convey the sense that you can handle all the complexities of managing the deal, from financing to due diligence and closing. Your advance preparation in researching the industry and type of company you plan to buy all increase the likelihood that people will view you as having what it takes to close the deal. In short, people have to believe that you are able to do the deal.

Your Educational Background and Work Experience. Formal education and work experience also contribute to your image. Others probably weigh your education more heavily in assessing your ability if you are younger. As you get older, work experience typically matters more.

Experience may be in a wide variety of business or technical professions, with engineering, sales, or finance being especially helpful. Any experience you may have working with banks is also helpful, even for a past personal loan such as a home mortgage.

Having an Initial Plan. Having a clear idea about what you want to do also builds confidence in others that you are able to complete the deal. A well-written business plan is also very helpful.

Your Business Associates The credibility of each of your business associates—investors, bankers, consultants, or employees—rubs off on your own image, for better or for worse. Especially if you are young, finding more seasoned members of the team can be very helpful in building credibility and in increasing the odds of your success. Be especially careful to look into the backgrounds of strangers. You do not want to ruin your own reputation by dealing with unscrupulous individuals, either as investors, lenders, employees, or business partners.

Credibility for a Particular Venture Credibility also varies depending upon the particular business venture you are embarking upon. Experience in one industry may or may not carry over fully into another industry. If you have experience in the manufacturing sector, for instance, you may still have to reestablish yourself in the service sector. Or if you have experience building diversified conglomerates in related industries, you may still have to establish credibility for success in building a portfolio for a holding company.

Credibility is Important in Deal Making

A credible image is essential at each stage in the deal-making process and for each group you may work with. For instance, in the early stages of searching for a company, credibility must be established with a banker so that you can obtain a letter of understanding, a document that indicates that a bank is willing to deal with you if you find the right company. The letter of understanding, in turn, helps you to obtain credibility with the broker community, which you need in order to obtain the lead flow to find the right deal. If you need other investors to raise sufficient capital for the deal, credibility is also essential with that group.

Credibility with the seller is also important. Whereas in real estate, a seller often has a contractual obligation with a listing broker to sell his or her property if a full price, cash, noncontingent offer is presented. Such requirements are rare in the sale of most businesses. Sellers have been known to refuse a sale to a higher bidder. Purchase of a company is a fairly complicated and drawn-out process. A seller is likely to back out of a deal or refuse to enter into one at all with a buyer that he or she does not trust. Where an investment banker screens initial prospects, you may not even have the opportunity to learn about or bid on a company unless the banker feels you are a legitimate buyer.

Finally, at later stages in the deal-making process, you will need to be viewed as trustworthy and believable by prospective employees. Otherwise, the value of the company you are purchasing may seriously erode before you even have a chance to take over due to a drop in productivity or increased turnover of valued employees.

Credibility and the Banker

Establishing credibility with the banker is often a prerequisite for establishing credibility with other parties. When you have established credibility with a bank, it will often provide you with a letter of understanding, which can be shown to the broker, seller, or others to show that a bank is likely to lend you money needed to close the deal. Although the bank is unlikely to provide you with a blanket approval, it will often provide such a letter on a deal-by-deal basis. This allows you to say to the seller, for instance, that he or she can call John Doe at First Bank to personally verify the relationship.

This was done when J.P. Industries was founded. Founder and author Psarouthakis spoke with representatives from a couple of investment banks and came to an understanding on a deal-by-deal basis. They gave permission to use their name in the brochure that J.P. Industries distributed to business brokers and potential sellers.

The banker is likely to consider the following issues in considering your credibility:

1. How serious are you about the business deal?
2. What are your qualifications for running the business?
3. What are your strategic thoughts? How are you going to be equally or more successful than the present owner of the company?
4. How much equity is available?
5. Who are the equity investors? Are you alone or are there others?
6. Do you have an initial business plan? and
7. Do you have a plan for paying off the loan?

How Serious You Are About Business Ownership

One way to establish the seriousness of your intent is the amount of effort you expend toward your new venture. In general, bankers and others assume that you are more serious about the project if you are working at it full-time. This is not to say that you must quit your present job to get a loan, but it does contribute to a banker's opinion of how serious you are about the project. A banker is likely to view you differently if you have two years of income saved up and are planning to look for companies full-time than if you are simply between jobs, or you are still working at your present job.

If you do plan to quit your job, you must plan for this step very carefully. You should be ready to live on savings for up to two years until you have made the transition to your new company. You also need to make plans with your family so that they are prepared and willing to make the appropriate sacrifices.

Your Business Qualifications for Running the Business

Though not necessary, it is helpful to have an master of business administration (MBA). During the acquisition process, having the MBA does have some impact. With or without the MBA, it is important to have good advisors. Your familiarity with the industry is also very important, not only to the banker but to the seller too. Many sellers feel uncomfortable with the "whiz kid" from Wall Street and would often rather deal with someone with past operating experience in the same or a related industry.

Your Strategic Thoughts

The banker will also want to know what you plan to do with your company. Do you know how you are going to improve value of the company and what you plan to do with the company in the long run? Why do you feel that an investment in this industry is a good move at this time and what changes will you make to assure that your company will be successful? Strategy doesn't need to be complicated, but it should be clearly thought out and communicated, preferably in a written business plan.

The Amount of Equity Available

Bankers frequently inform all those who will listen that they are not in the equity business. They expect a significant percentage of the transaction will be covered by equity investment by you or other investors. The rule of thumb varies from year to year and decade to decade and industry to industry. For instance, in manufacturing, today, a typical ratio is $3 of debt to $1 of equity depending upon the degree to which the loan can be secured by tangible assets within the company. Although much more highly leveraged acquisitions with ratios as high as ten or twelve have been supported by banks in the past, their high failure rate has made most banks more cautious. The ratio will vary from bank to bank and also from industry to industry, typically being much lower for a service-type business lacking inventory or other assets to secure the loan.

The Other Equity Investors, If Any

Your investment group can contribute substantially to your credibility with the banker, seller, brokers, and others. If someone with wealth has made a significant investment in your project, this definitely contributes to your credibility.

Your Initial Business Plan

Adequate attention to the development of an initial business plan will assist in building credibility with the banker. The banker wants to be sure you have a clear idea of what type of company you are looking for, what you are going to do with that company once you buy it (fix it up for resale, create a group of companies, etc.), and how you are going to go about finding the right company and making the deal (how you will find the leads, who will assist you in screening the right candidates, how you will carry out due diligence, and so forth). Once you identify the specific company you plan to buy, you will then need to prepare a more detailed plan for that company.

Your Plan to Pay Off the Loan

The banker will want to know how you plan to pay off the loan. For instance, do you plan to go public, sell the company, or simply pay off the loan from cash flow? The banker wants to know what they will get in return for the risk they are taking.

The Extent to Which the Loan Can Be Secured

You don't necessarily have to be an executive from a *Fortune 500* company to get a bank loan. The bank will evaluate the assets of the company you plan to purchase. As alluded to earlier, a banker will feel more comfortable lending to you if you have some way of securing the debt, whether with personal assets, assets from your existing business, if you have one, or assets of the company that you plan to purchase.

Credibility and the Investor

Many of the same issues described already that contribute to credibility for the banker and seller are also likely to pertain to the investor. In addition, the investor will want to know the exit strategy for his or her investment, which may or may not be the same plan as for the banker. For instance, if you take the company public, this might be a way to pay off both the banker and investor. Or you may plan to pay the investor with a high level of dividend distribution of earnings.

Credibility and the Broker

Companies are bought and sold in a very unique way, compared with any other industry. There are few publicly available places to find out about which businesses are for sale because it is usually not in a company's best interest to advertise broadly that it is on the market. Existing customers, suppliers, and employees may become apprehensive about a potential change in ownership. And some leads are only developed by brokers after it becomes evident that a potential buyer might be interested in a particular firm. Many companies are sold each year that their owners had not even considered selling at the outset, but after hard work by a broker and expressed interest by a buyer, eventually a deal was made. Brokers do not pursue such leads for a buyer unless they feel that the buyer is serious and capable of following through with the purchase.

Some general factors related to credibility concern your educational background, your advisors, and experience. If you have an MBA, good advisors, and familiarity with the industry you are going into, you are likely to establish credibility more easily with brokers as well as with other groups.

Credibility with the banker also helps you to establish credibility with the broker community. Obtaining a letter of understanding from the banker can be very useful in establishing that credibility. Thus, all the issues related to credibility with the banker apply here as well.

Credibility and the Seller

The seller has to feel that you can make the deal. Five things are important to the seller in determining credibility:

1. Can you finance the deal?
2. How serious are you about making a deal?
3. Do you know how to make the deal?
4. Will you treat employees fairly?
5. Do you plan to retain the integrity of the original business?

Your Ability to Finance the Deal

Generally, the seller doesn't want to wait a year while you find the money. The *rare* seller will give you six months to find the money. Most sellers realize you may not have the cash in the bank, but they want to feel comfortable that having made the deal, you can get access to the money almost immediately. You need to assure the seller that you have serious money sources subject to the deal. Then he will be comfortable dealing with you because the financing is obviously there. You should develop a strong relationship and obtain a letter of understanding from at least one bank early on in your search. You also need to line up whichever equity sources you might require.

How Serious You Are About Making a Deal

How serious you are about making the deal is often determined by others by the commitment you have made to the search. In addition to having the funds required, awareness of the time and effort involved is important for credibility not only with the seller but with business brokers. Whether fairly interpreted or not, most in the deal-making business will take a buyer less seriously who is still working at a full-time job or who comes across as being "between jobs" and just looking around. Making a deal is a demanding process that requires full-time attention to see through in a reasonable amount of time. You need to plan for as much as eighteen months to two years to see a search through from beginning to end. About one year is to find the right company. Figure another six to ten months to complete the acquisition process once you find the right company.

Your Knowledge of the Deal-Making Process

Making the right deal requires knowledge of the different business functions, including marketing, finance, accounting, legal and operational aspects of the business as well as technical aspects related to the particular industry. In addition, you will need all the specific deal-making skills, including evaluating, pricing, valuing, and negotiating the possible deal as well as closing the final deal.

Your Likely Treatment of Employees

Your perceived treatment of future employees is often a concern in the family business, especially where many employees have worked in the company for many years.

Your Long-Term Plans for the Company

Many sellers, especially the owner of a private company who has spent a lifetime building the business, want to feel that you are not planning to hack the company to pieces as soon as you have bought it. These same sellers may be concerned about whether you plan to move the company to another city or otherwise destroy the identity or integrity of the original business. These concerns are likely to be less for the large conglomerate selling off a division. However, to the extent it might impact employee relations at the remaining company, it can still be important.

Credibility with Other Groups

The issue of credibility with customers and suppliers is not as critical as it is with the aforementioned groups, at least in the early stages, and for larger companies. However, it may be of concern in small companies. The customer will be concerned with the continuity of services. Suppliers are concerned that they are going to lose you.

The employee issue, although not an issue early on in the negotiations, can be very important in later stages. Whenever ownership changes, people may feel a great degree of uncertainty. Uncertainty creates insecurities, and insecurities can create low productivity. You may lose your good people before the deal closes. So you need to move quickly even during the due diligence phase as the rumor of a possible sale of the company spreads among employees. You also need to relate with employees so that they can begin to know you. It is important to communicate who you are, why you bought the company, and in broad terms, what you plan to do with the company.

Credibility with the public can be a factor, especially with a large publicly-held company. They will want to know your plans for the company as well, especially plans that will dramatically increase or decrease the number of jobs that your company provides the local community. Plant closings, expansions, or other abrupt changes in employment levels will be of great concern.

Chapter Summary

Credibility is a very important aspect of success in purchasing a company. Many of the issues important to establishment of credibility for one constituency may also apply to some of the other groups. Looked at altogether, the following issues are likely to help you to establish trustworthiness and believability in your proposed venture with the business community and the community at large:

1. That you are serious enough about making the deal that you are devoting significant resources and effort to this venture. If you are a first-time buyer, full-time dedication to this venture will contribute positively to your image.
2. That you have reasonable qualifications for running the business, such as an MBA, appropriate work experience in a related industry and/or directly transferable management experience.
3. That you are clear about your vision for the company and can communicate why you will be more successful than the present owner in the case of an underperforming firm or at least as successful as the present owner in a well-performing firm.
4. That when approaching the bank for a loan, you have the necessary amount of equity to support the loan.
5. That you have equity partners who are considered credible themselves, either as savvy, experienced businesspeople and/or as investors in previously successful deals.
6. That you have a plan for paying off the loan, either through cash flow from the company, by eventually selling the company for a profit, or by taking the company public.
7. That you have an exit strategy for investors, which will provide them with a significant return on their investment.
8. That you are able to finance the deal, usually evidenced by a letter of understanding from the bank.
9. That you know how to make the deal, showing a clear understanding of the different steps needed to conclude the sale.
10. That, especially in the case of the seller, you will treat employees fairly and

11. That you are able to communicate clearly to bankers, brokers, employees, and others, what you plan to do and how you plan to do it. This should include an initial business plan that clearly spells out why you are doing this, what type of business you plan to buy, and how you plan to find the right company.

CHAPTER 5

BUILDING THE ACQUISITION TEAM

No one person is likely to have expertise in all the areas required to make a thorough evaluation of business prospects. You need to bring advisors on board early on, whether as part-time consultants or as employees, to provide you with the expertise you will need to effectively screen different business opportunities.

Why You Need a Team

Some books may recommend that you take shortcuts in screening business opportunities. We firmly believe, based on personal experience and available research, that you cannot afford to cut corners in obtaining sound advice before closing the deal. If you do, you may save several thousand dollars in the short run, but if you plan to invest your life savings or other large sums of money into what proves to be a money-losing proposition, you have lost much more money in the long run taking such shortcuts.

If you develop an initial business plan that clearly spells out *what* you want to do and *how* you want to do it and establish appropriate credibility, then you are more likely to raise some of the money you need to build the team. It's an issue of approach, not one of sophistication.

Financing the Team

In the beginning, you are not likely to get a bank loan for your search unless you take out a personal loan. Start with family, friends, or acquaintances that are relatively easy to access. They will network you further, and then, you might go to professional institutions. Generally, start-up costs to cover the screening and evaluation costs of different business prospects come from an immediate circle of friends.

Most consultants are unwilling to work for free at this stage, but they might be willing to give you a lower rate.

Characteristics of a Good Team

A good team is made up of several people who have their own area of expertise but who function together as a team. Each of them looks at their own area of competence and integrates it in cross-functional discussions. A good team is composed of competent individuals who understand the importance of working together with others.

Beware of the trap that many entrepreneurs fall into—that they want to do it all by themselves. The risk is that you don't know what you are doing. Your venture has a much higher risk of failure than when you involve professionals to help you evaluate prospects, even though your up-front expenses are higher. An entrepreneur makes a big mistake who thinks he can handle everything without expert help.

You should not proceed to buy a business if you cannot afford a lawyer or an accountant who can evaluate the appropriate aspects of the business.

The Attorney: Your First Player

Very few deals can get by without the services of an experienced, competent lawyer. The attorney provides support in several key areas:

1. To articulate understandings with the seller
2. To assure conformance with Securities and Exchange Commission regulations for investors
3. To assure conformance in the sale process with various government regulations such as anti-trust law, regulations, and taxes
4. To assure compliance by the prospective company with various regulations and laws

Consult an attorney to articulate and interpret understandings with the seller.

Your negotiations begin at the moment you make initial contact with either the seller or broker about a particular lead. This contact may set the mood or atmosphere for negotiations throughout the process. Therefore, you are wise to bring in an attorney very early in the game, preferably at the very start before you contact brokers to express interest about specific opportunities.

You also need an attorney to help with the various legal documents that put these understandings on paper. For example, you are likely to be asked to sign a confidentiality agreement before you are even given the name of a prospective company for sale. You should not sign any document, not even the confidentiality agreement, without an attorney's review in order to avoid unwanted understandings and legal repercussions further along into the process. A good lawyer can help you to prevent future problems. It is important not to make errors, legally speaking, that may complicate the process by accidentally setting up an understanding that complicates the contract from a legal point of view. For example, you can write in a letter that this is not a binding proposal and is only an expression of interest but still find out that in that letter, there may still be agreements considered binding under the law. For instance, if one of the parties walks out arbitrarily, he may be obligated, nevertheless, to compensate the other party. Even though the letter says it is not binding, this paragraph remains binding unless it is spelled out in the proper manner. In sum, if you don't want expensive surprises down the line, you are wise to obtain legal services at the start.

Consult an attorney to assure conformance with Securities and Exchange Commission regulations for investors.

You also need to consult with a good attorney before raising funds from private investors. For instance, in the U.S., the Securities and Exchange Commission tightly regulates the manner in which potential investors can be solicited, depending upon a wide range of parameters that your attorney will be familiar with. The number and type of investors is strictly regulated depending upon the legal structure that you have chosen for your business.

Consult an attorney to assure compliance by the prospective company with various regulations and laws.

Another very important aspect of your attorney's work arises during due diligence. He or she should be skilled in this type of activity, knowing what types of potential problems to look for and documents to review.

What to look for in legal help

Attorneys vary widely in their backgrounds and experience. It is best to obtain an attorney, first and foremost, experienced with the purchase and sale of companies, who is familiar with such documents as the letter of interest, letter of intent, due diligence, closing documents, and so forth. Secondly, if you can locate an attorney who specializes in a particular industry, such as for instance radio/communication deals or international deals, you will likely save money and get better service in the long run even if you have to pay a slightly higher hourly rate to do so.

Other Members of the Team

In addition to a good attorney, you are likely to need the assistance of at least one accountant to help you develop your business plan and an auditor to review the seller's books. Sometimes this is the same individual, but in a larger acquisition, it may require two different people. You may also need someone skilled in arranging financing and depending upon your own business background, one or more consultants in sales and marketing, operations, engineering, and manufacturing. If real property is involved, you are very likely to need the help of an environmental consultant.

These advisors may remain as consultants or eventually become part of your management team. If multiple partners are involved with the acquisition, then it is possible that some of them may play a role, either initially or long-term, in these areas. What is important is the access to competent advice in each area early on in the acquisition process.

The Accountant

In addition to an attorney, every deal also requires the assistance of a good accountant who will be needed at different stages in the process:

1. To audit or evaluate financial statements and other documents to assess the financial condition of the prospective company
2. To help develop pro forma statements for your business plan once you identify a prospect to purchase including planning cost analysis

The Financial Consultant

In addition to your accountant, you will find it helpful or necessary to obtain a consultant who specializes in advice in raising money. At J.P. Industries, the initial team included both an accountant and a person skilled in finance. Investment bankers often offer this service, together with direct help in raising the capital required. Investment bankers are becoming increasingly involved in this way, especially for larger deals.

Sales and Marketing

Sales and marketing have always been important, but in today's market-driven economy, it is essential to have someone familiar with this area to evaluate companies under consideration for acquisition. You will want someone on your team who understands market strategy and dynamics as well as other marketing-related issues such as distribution and pricing. You also need someone expert in market strategy who can evaluate the health of the niche that your prospective companies serve. You may have such experience, especially if you have a strong marketing and strategic background. If not, you will need to seek out an experienced marketing manager or marketing consultant to advise you.

Operations, Engineering, and Manufacturing

Manufacturing firms also need team members capable of evaluating the engineering and manufacturing aspects of prospective deals. Several issues relate to the condition and quality of the facilities and equipment. Are they in good repair? Are they up-to-date? Both software and hardware capabilities need to be assessed. For instance, in engineering design, does the company have computer-aided design (CAD) capability? Is the production process laid out efficiently? Are engineering and manufacturing working together for new products? Is the company able to design and make its own production tooling, or is this subcontracted out? Who controls the know-how and the tools? Are the tools designed well, technically speaking, in terms of longevity or maintenance requirements? After a certain number of parts produced, who maintains them? If inventory is a significant part of the business, careful valuation of the inventory will need to take place before the price can be determined. Do inventory items move quickly, or are some items going to need to be written off? Is there too much or too little inventory in vital areas? Are modern inventory control and ordering techniques in use? These and many other questions can be answered by the appropriate engineering consultant or team member with engineering and/or appropriate operations background. But it is vital that you identify someone capable of evaluating this area to assess whether it is technically current.

The Environmental Consultant

The environmental consultant is an essential consultant in any deal that involves real property. A preliminary inspection can often be done fairly inexpensively to identify whether more extensive testing is needed. The owner may be unaware of potential problems. In the case of one company explored by JPE Inc., an underground tank had been removed and had covered the foundation of a new factory floor several years previously. Unfortunately, the tank had leaked before it had been removed and had created a modest pollution problem, which nevertheless could be somewhat costly to clean up. You need to locate a consultant that specifically specializes in testing for standards set by the appropriate governmental agency, such as the United States Environmental Protection Agency.

Putting the Team Together

Even if people have their own area of expertise, they have to function together as a team. Each of them looks at their own area of competence and integrates it in cross-functional discussions. A good team is composed of competent individuals who understand the importance of working together with others.

Where to Find Prospective Team Members

This is one of the difficult challenges faced by all growing ventures, even after the launch of the start-up phase. Word-of-mouth recommendations from other business associates who have had success, contacts you have made in past work experiences, and formal referrals from other consultants are some of the possible sources. In a community, competent service providers will often know of other people that they have worked with in other deals and situations. One advantage of working with everyone on your team initially as a consultant is that the commitment is more short-term in nature. This gives you the opportunity to observe that person's competence and fit with the team before making a long-term commitment. You may sift through several deals before you close on a particular company. Contract on a short-term, deal-by-deal basis if you are not sure how adequately a particular consultant may service your needs until you get to know them and whether they fit your expectations.

Chapter Summary

Building a good team is important right at the outset of your search. You will need an attorney almost immediately to review any confidentiality agreements or letters of interest that must be signed. However, you should also begin to think about the other team members you will need early on in the search process. A good accountant is essential to the adequate review of the seller's books, and possibly in addition, an independent auditor. Other consultants you need may depend upon your own skill levels and the nature of the business. If you will need outside funding, a financial consultant may be needed. Depending upon your own background in the functional business areas of sales and marketing, operations, engineering, and manufacturing, you may or may not require outside help. An environmental consultant is increasingly needed whenever real property is involved in the transaction to assure that no hidden problems exist.

Be sure that you investigate any strangers thoroughly to assure that they have the competence that you expect and to avoid the chance of involving the unscrupulous. Referrals from trusted acquaintances that have used someone in the past is ideal, but if you do not have such contacts, check out others as thoroughly as you can. It is also important that team members work together smoothly that they are able to communicate well and to treat each other with respect.

CHAPTER 6

CASTING THE NET FOR BUSINESS LEADS

You might just stumble upon the business of your future at a cocktail party or through a friend or family contact. This happens. But statistically, this does not happen very frequently. The majority of successful business purchases are found by culling dozens, if not hundreds of business opportunities. And those business opportunities flow from a broad network of sources. This chapter describes the means by which you develop your lead flow, an essential step in finding the right business to buy.

The Concept of the Lead Flow

To find the ideal company to purchase, you may need to look at hundreds of prospects on paper. You whittle these down to the few you see in person to a smaller number that you negotiate and then finally to that one that you buy. You are not going to amass these leads all at once. It is more constructive to think of this process as a lead flow as we presented in figure 1-1. You can create this flow by developing a network of brokers and other business contacts that feed you leads over time. Then, you review leads as they come to you. To find the ideal company, you want to keep the lead flow going until your sale is closed. You might find a company far more suited to your needs than the one you are currently negotiating, and it is important not to get locked into the final sale any time before you actually close the deal.

The Business Broker: Key to the Search

You can obtain leads from many different sources. Some may come from friends and family. In the well-organized search, most are likely to come from brokers whose livelihood is the identification of businesses for sale. These brokers cannot be found in the Yellow Pages and vary in sophistication. Most first-time buyers will need about ten active finders—those sending you leads on a regular basis to obtain the necessary lead flow. Over time you can build up your contacts. More experienced buyers may eventually accumulate a list of several hundred finders but even so may have about a dozen finders actively sending leads for them at any one time. However, the group changes constantly. To assure a continuous flow of leads, you need to keep up your contacts with existing finders while adding new finders to your list throughout the search process.

Types of Brokers

Most business brokers you will encounter fit into one of two broad categories—the *investment banker*, who is usually paid by and represents the seller directly and the *finder*, a broker, who seeks out or "finds" prospects for individuals interested in buying a company. The finder is also referred to as an "intermediary" or a "go-between" between buyer and seller.

There are both similarities and differences in working with the various types of business brokers. Your credibility is key to any broker. Few brokers will waste their time sending you leads if they have doubts about your knowledge and ability to make a deal since they almost all operate on a commission paid either by the seller or the buyer, if the deal is closed. The broker will do a lot of work for you once he or she perceives that you are a live candidate, however, with the knowledge, ability, and desire to close.

Public companies divesting a division are apt to hire an investment banker as do larger companies, typically of at least $50 million in sales.

The investment banker provides expert valuation and greater credibility to a board of directors that a fair deal has taken place. However, investment bankers are costly to the seller and furthermore, often will not bother with small to medium-sized companies, even many of those operating at levels of $20 million in sales or more. Thus, you are likely to locate most small to medium-sized businesses, other than divisions of larger companies with the aid of a finder.

You are also likely to encounter differences in the expectations, legal documents, and procedures among different types of brokers. The next section describes the experiences you are likely to encounter with different types of brokers.

The Investment Banker

The investment banker is the most sophisticated type of broker. If you encounter an investment-banker managed deal, you can expect fairly similar procedures. Investment bankers are retained by a prospective seller in this situation. Thus, when the source of your lead is an investment banker, you can safely assume that you are dealing with a committed seller. The seller has already incurred considerable expense and time with the investment banker to have a "book" assembled and would not likely go to such expense unless he or she was serious about selling the company. A "book" is a report prepared by the investment banker, which contains fairly detailed historical and financial information about the company, market information, and other background information about the company being sold. This book is prepared before anyone is even contacted that the company is for sale. Considerable time is spent in polishing the financial statements, adjusting the extraordinary expenses, such as excess salaries for the owner or above market rents for leased property to show a normalized profit and loss statement.

As a prospective buyer, you cannot automatically receive the book about a company for sale. Regardless of who contacts you, the initial information you receive is likely to be rather limited and general. If the investment banker is already aware of your interest in buying similar companies, he or she may contact you directly by phone or letter. Or you may receive a one-page description of the company from another broker. This one-page description may identify the location, type of industry and size in rather general terms, e.g., a Midwest manufacturer of gaskets supplying the auto industry between $10 and $20 million in revenues. The name of the company and precise descriptions are not given to avoid gossip. To receive "the book," you will be required to sign and return a confidentiality agreement.

When dealing with a lead from an investment banker, you will have to sign a letter of interest, which includes an estimate of the price you are willing to pay, before you are allowed to meet the seller and visit the company for sale. The letter of interest is used by the investment banker to screen out the people who are going to offer too low a price or who aren't going to be able to make the deal. It is almost like an auction. Typically, only about six or seven buyers are invited to meet with the seller and the setting is much more formal than with other types of leads. When dealing with a lead from an investment banker, you can also expect that the investment banker will want to stay heavily involved with the transaction throughout the deal process. This can be somewhat problematic because both successful evaluation and negotiation of a deal depend upon extensive contact with the seller. The seller will often reveal information that you cannot obtain in reports or from other people. However, be persistent in seeking out opportunities to meet with the seller, preferably directly and alone, and you will find them, even when the investment banker is involved with the deal.

The Finder

Unlike investment bankers, among finders you are likely to encounter much more variation in the process. Finders may have a full-time service business or may be a semi-retired executive working out of his or her home. Although it is probably more accurate to view these finders along a continuum, for the sake of discussion, we will divide finders into two subclassifications—the *professional broker* and the *informal intermediary* to point out some typical differences you might encounter working with various brokers.

Almost all finders require that a *fee agreement* be signed before they send you any leads. A fee agreement is an agreement between buyer and broker where the buyer agrees to pay a fee contingent on the closing of a deal. No expense is incurred otherwise.

The professional broker Somewhere between the very informal intermediary and the sophisticated investment broker is the professional intermediary broker. This type of finder usually has an office outside the home and one or more employees assisting him or her. In spite of their more formal status, these people are still not easy to identify. They are not licensed in most states. They are not listed in the Yellow Pages. However, as a group, they also account for a significant proportion of the leads that actually get executed into sales.

You can expect the professional intermediary to gather a fair amount of information for you once he or she has a fee agreement with you. You can expect to receive financial statements, product literature, and a two- or three-page summary of the business before visiting the company up for sale. You can expect leads from this source to be screened by the finder so that the company is actually for sale. By contrast, among the more informal intermediaries, often what you get is little more than a lead that you have to invest time exploring further.

Once you make contact with the seller, however, the professional broker tends to take a backseat on the process, unlike the investment banker. Most of them would prefer to spend their time looking for another deal hoping nevertheless that one day they will receive a check for their matchmaking efforts. This is actually quite helpful because it allows easier access between buyer and seller during the evaluation and negotiation process than when the broker remains involved.

The informal intermediary At the other end of the spectrum is the informal intermediary, another type of finder that works for the buyer. The informal intermediary may only close one or two companies per year.

Some informal intermediaries bring you leads on the basis of a telephone conversation with the prospective seller or on the basis of a seller's response to a finder's letter. Or he may drive around town, making cold calls to business owners. Again, though, expect to sign a fee agreement before the intermediary does much work for you.

Your first contact from the informal intermediary is likely to be a phone call or an e-mail rather than a letter or other written information. The finder may not even know whether or not the company is really for sale but is calling to find out whether the particular company is the sort you might be interested in. When the lead is first generated, the informal intermediary usually has much less information available to both himself and to the buyer than other brokers might. He probably has an estimate of total revenues and whether or not the company is profitable. If he has actually visited the company, he may also have a brief description of the site. There is no book or organized gathering of information. The finder is not likely to tell you even where the company is located until you have signed a fee agreement and a confidentiality agreement. Don't be surprised, however, if the finder asks you to provide your own form for the confidentiality agreement. Some finders do not always keep such forms on hand.

If the lead meets your initial broad criteria, then you should indicate a possible interest. Once you have expressed initial interest, typically, this type of finder will want to set up a face-to-face meeting with the owner before providing you with detailed information. This is very different from the investment banker who will only present a limited number of buyers to the seller based on a letter of interest. In this situation, the intermediary might not even be present at the first meeting between buyer and seller. At that first meeting, the buyer should not be surprised to discover that the seller is not interested in selling his company after all! But it would be a mistake to exclude review of such leads because many sales are consummated from just such informal contacts made by such brokers.

Though partly true of all brokers, the informal intermediary is quite likely to lose interest very quickly without continuing contact and feedback from the buyer. He or she might make a few phone contacts and forget about you unless you keep reminding him of your interest. The simplest approach is to set up a database from which you can send a regular mailing to all brokers on your list to keep them aware of your current interests. It may seem like a lot of effort, but it is important to keep in mind that many good deals often arise from this source.

As quirky as some of them are at times, these informal intermediaries are your bread and butter. The investment banker may never have heard of the companies that your finders uncover. If the finder knows you're committed, that you have the money and the know-how to do a deal, he will go out and work for you.

Other Types of Business Broker

Whereas finders are hired by the buyer, some business brokers other than investment bankers are hired by the seller. Other brokers may alternately work for either a buyer or seller over time.

Other Sources of Leads

Although in our view, the best and most plentiful source of leads will be derived from your broker network, you may also want to explore some other sources of leads. Some buyers learn about businesses for sale through their network of bankers, attorneys, and accountants. But these are often weak business prospects. In the banker's case, you must beware that the bank may be trying to sell the company in order to retrieve its own assets. The bank may not get paid unless the company is sold.

A more productive way of viewing alternative sources of leads is as a means of tracking down business brokers. This idea is explained further in the next section.

Locating the Business Broker

Many investment bankers are well-known and can be easily identified. Finding the intermediary or finder requires far greater effort because they do not generally advertise their services nor are they listed in the Yellow Pages. This section describes some ways you can begin to develop your own list.

Locating business brokers through other business professionals Your own attorney, accountant, or banker might not be the best or most direct source of qualified leads, but he or she may have the names of some finders that you can contact. Try to locate other professional support people in your community who are involved with acquisition activity. They are quite likely to have names of at least a few finders from their own past dealings.

Responding to newspaper ads One of the most useful ways to identify brokers is to respond to an ad in the *Wall Street Journal* for a company that is for sale. Quite often, you will get an intermediary's name. Then you can add that broker's name to the list even if you are not interested in the particular company being advertised.

Placing an ad in a business newspaper Though more expensive, you can also locate brokers by placing your own ad in the *Wall Street Journal*, *New York Times* or the business section of your regional newspaper, expressing your interest in acquiring a company. The ad might read like this:

> "Acquisition wanted in the computer services business, sales up to $10 million, located preferably in _____ (location), financing available (if it is). Please contact ABC company, Mr. _____, (your telephone number), (your fax)."

With this type of ad, you are not likely to get responses from owners. But you are likely to be contacted by brokers who might otherwise be difficult to ferret out. When brokers respond, they usually tell you more about themselves, and you can tell them more about what you are looking for. In our experience at JPE, when we ran an ad in the *Wall Street Journal*, about nine out of ten responses were intermediaries.

Contacting a professional association of brokers A growing number of business intermediaries belong to a professional association. The Association for Corporate Growth (ACG), one such organization, is a US organization whose members are involved primarily with corporate growth via acquisition. Many of its members are intermediaries. Such organizations may provide you with a list of finders and brokers.

Building Credibility with the Business Broker

Several factors contribute to your credibility with the broker, regardless of his or her sophistication. The most important are as follows:

1. You are clear about what you are looking for. Ideally, you should have acquisition criteria that are written and spelled out.
2. You understand and are committed to the buying process.
3. You have the financial capability to close.
4. Credibility is critical in the relationship between buyer and broker because without it, the broker is not likely to bother to provide you with leads.

Making and Maintaining Contact with a Business Broker

Once you identify the name of a business broker, you can contact him either by telephone to tell him who you are and what you are looking for. It is helpful to acknowledge up front that there will be a mutually agreed fee and that you are looking forward to his input. Subsequently, whenever a finder sends you a lead, it is important to respond quickly and courteously, or he will stop contacting you. Your response should indicate whether or not a lead meets your criteria, your appreciation for the time taken to send you the lead even if it doesn't fit your needs, and finally, an indication that you hope the broker will continue to send you leads in the future. In the event that the initial information you receive from a broker is too sketchy to make a decision, request additional information rather than reject the lead out of hand.

Remember that most brokers work on commission. They will spend time on their most likely prospects. They are not obligated to serve you. You must stay in frequent contact with a finder if you expect him or her to keep looking. If you follow the recommended guidelines, a finder is more likely to continue sending you prospects even though you may not buy anything from him or her for several months or even years. But if he gets the impression that you may never get in touch with him, he will question the worth of investing his time or money on you. A finder knows that you are not going to buy a company from every finder but if they feel you are a serious buyer, that you behave professionally, and occasionally you buy a company, the finder will remain in touch over a long period.

In addition to responding to particular leads, you should keep in touch with your broker network through regular mailings, phone contacts, and for some of the more active finders, an occasional lunch. For instance, you should send "your" brokers press releases on a regular basis, and otherwise, keep them abreast of what you are doing. At any given time, you may only have a dozen intermediaries actively looking for you, but the particular group contacting you changes over time. You or one of your team should maintain more direct contact with the most promising of these brokers, by calling them periodically and even taking them out to lunch. This helps to keep them fired up and enthusiastic.

What to Expect from "Your" Broker

Although you try to cast as wide a net as possible in the beginning, once your leads really begin to flow, you will need to filter out unwanted leads—and brokers that appear to waste your time on a chronic basis. Due to confidentiality concerns, most leads first arrive to you with very limited information. Initially, you try to use your acquisition criteria to select the leads you want to pursue. But as mentioned, you may have to invest additional time in gathering information before you even have enough information to compare with your initial screening criteria. In order to make most efficient use of your own time, you may find that some brokers should be dropped from your list because they are wasting your time. Two common problems to alert yourself to, are the brokers who (1) keep sending you irrelevant leads, and/or (2) keep sending you poorly qualified leads.

The broker who sends irrelevant leads. Some brokers do not take the time or interest to understand the criteria that you have set up. Of course, if you do not clearly communicate your own needs in the beginning, you cannot expect all the leads a broker sends to be appropriate to your needs. But if you have outlined your needs, say for instance, you are seeking a manufacturing firm, and your broker keeps sending you leads in retail and service areas, he or she is wasting your valuable time. A good broker will take the time to learn about your needs and prescreen the leads he or she receives, only sending you the relevant ones.

The broker who sends poorly qualified leads Poor qualification of leads is a second common problem, especially among the informal intermediaries. These finders may be on a "fishing expedition" with the seller, and may even send you leads from owners who have no intention at all of selling their companies. They may send you a lead to determine the type of business you are interested in and then try to interest the seller in meeting with you. This type of broker isn't as problematic as the first unless the intermediary involves you in the process, having you meet with the owner only to find out that he or she is not interested in selling, at least not for a reasonable price. One way to spot this type of finder is if he has a hard time providing you with any information about the company before your first meeting with the seller.

Learning who your credible brokers are, the ones who send you helpful leads, is especially important in determining follow-up of leads that are very limited in initial information. For instance, a broker may contact you with a lead in the appropriate size and profit range but you have no idea what industry it is in or what products it makes. If the broker says that this is something he thinks you would be interested in, you have to evaluate the source. Is this a serious broker who knows your criteria and is there some reason for him or her not to tell you what it is, or is this a broker who is just wasting your time? One way to respond, if you are not sure about the broker, is to provide the following answer:

> "Thank you for sending us this brief description of the prospect that you represent. It certainly meets our sales and profitability criteria, but before we go any further, we would like to know what products they have or what industry they are in."

You may not get an answer to this query without being asked to sign a confidentiality agreement and a fee agreement. At that point, you have to decide whether or not you are dealing with a serious finder. For instance, has this person sent you good leads before? Or if its someone new, has he sent you a nicely-put-together document for the confidentiality agreement, or is it on a handwritten piece of paper?

One thing to keep in mind is that you will be dealing with a lot of volume as your lead flow begins to build. Along the way, you will make mistakes but you shouldn't worry about it. You may turn off a deal that could be great, but at the same time, you don't want to go too far because you don't have enough information.

If you do keep getting irrelevant leads from a particular broker, you don't really want to tell him directly that you don't want to deal with him unless he has done something unethical. Once you stop communicating with him, he will gradually stop contacting you anyway. Conversely, as we mentioned before, you need to maintain ongoing contact with brokers who are sending you helpful leads, or they will stop sending you leads as well.

More about Broker Commissions and Fees

Similar to real estate transactions, one or more brokers typically receive a commission in exchange for bringing the buyer and seller together. Technically speaking, in the case of the investment banker, the seller pays the fee. In the case of the finder, the buyer pays. Exhibit 6.1 presents a sample fee agreement between buyer and finder. The agreement establishes the amount and conditions upon which a fee is paid. Generally, a fee is paid only if a finder provides a prospect that leads to a sale. Although the broker often desires a blanket agreement, it is advisable to obtain a fee agreement that pertains to each particular lead. This reduces the chance of misunderstandings later about who is owed a commission for which leads.

Though not always agreed upon, some variation of the standard Lehman formula often forms the basis of the commission. Although the exact figures vary, the idea behind the formula is that the commission is based on a percentage of the total price of the transaction, and that percentage slides downward as the price increases. Thus, based on one variant of the formula, the buyer may pay 5% for up to the first million dollars of the price, 4% on the second million dollars, 3% on the third million, 2% on the fourth million and 1% for everything above that. Sometimes brokers may try to ask for a higher commission, for instance,

5% on the first two million dollars of the transaction. Others may give a price break for amounts above $5 million.

One might debate who really pays the fee. Whether an investment banker or intermediary helped with the deal, the fee has to be taken out of the transaction. Since the seller has a certain expectation of how much he wants to make on the deal, the fee often gets added into the final price of the deal even when the seller pays the commission up front. For instance, the buyer may agree to pay for an agreed-upon amount of liabilities for "putting the corporation into condition to sell the stock." This is a subtle way of saying the buyer will pay for the investment bankers' fees. Such an agreement is typically included in a letter of intent, and subsequently, in the purchase agreement.

In negotiating finder fees, it is helpful to clarify the role that a finder plays in the deal. For instance, one finder may search the bushes to find a company while another learns that a company is available for sale from an investment banker. The first broker has put a lot more effort into the sale and may deserve a larger commission. It is helpful, therefore to ask whether or not another investment broker is involved. If so, you might want to negotiate a finder's fee rate rather than a full commission if another broker is involved. This is not merely an issue of matching effort to reward on the part of the broker. As described above, if another broker is involved, you may indirectly end up paying that fee as well, even though officially, it is paid by the seller.

Finder's fees can vary but it is not unusual to negotiate a flat rate such as 1% to 2% of the total price, rather than the full Lehman formula, and it depends on the size of the deal. But there is no real standard in the industry. However, if the person has actually gone out and beat on doors looking for a prospective seller, it is reasonable to pay the standard Lehman formula.

Sometimes people question the amount of money a finder might make on any one deal. People sometimes ignore the amount of time and effort a finder puts in before a deal actually closes. The finder may send your company leads for years without getting paid. The good finder has obtained these leads by actually going out and looking for opportunities. He has to feel that he is going to score big because most of the time he does not. The informal intermediary may feel he or she is doing pretty well to close two or three deals per year.

How Leads Come in to You

As you start to build up your network of intermediaries, you will typically begin to get leads in one of three ways:

1. You may receive a phone call from an investment banker or intermediary. You should tell the broker then and there whether or not you have interest in pursuing it any further.
2. You may receive a one-page executive summary in the mail. It is important to respond to these leads. For leads you are not interested in, you should write the broker and tell him or her why the lead doesn't fit your criteria and if you would like that broker to continue sending you leads. You might be able to let some of these slip by without replying but the more you communicate, the better off you are.
3. Finally, you might receive a list of companies. For example, you may get a booklet with 100-150 companies for sale around the country from Geneva, a national organization, ranging from a drugstore chain to hopefully something that is relevant.

Especially if you include the booklets of leads, once you start gathering leads, you may have quite limited information on literally thousands of leads. Thus, it is important to keep your key criteria clearly in mind and only pursue those leads that fit your needs. Otherwise, you will get distracted by leads that are not likely to meet your needs. It is worth asking for follow-up information for those leads that meet your initial criteria for revenues, product information, and profitability. You are likely to have to sign a confidentiality agreement in order to receive any additional information.

Keeping Track of Your Leads

As you uncover leads that might be worthwhile, you should keep a record of each lead as long as it remains in your active file. You are likely to receive pieces of information about the company over time, perhaps

---

some facts via a written letter and additional information by telephone or from an initial visit with the owner. Even before embarking on your preliminary due diligence, it is useful to maintain a file for each lead so that you do not lose track of any opportunities.

One rule of thumb is to keep a file on any lead for which you have signed a confidentiality agreement and have not yet rejected. These leads are likely to be in varying stages of evaluation and negotiation, anything from those for which you have just signed a confidentiality agreement and have little more than a name to those in advanced stages of discussion for which you are carrying out formal due diligence.

A sample summary sheet, similar to the one used at JPE Inc. is shown in exhibit 6.2. You may want to design your own worksheet or develop some other database model. What is important is that you do not lose track of viable leads. Those leads are expensive to obtain, and you don't want to make the mistake of misplacing important information. You may want to develop clear rules for keeping a lead in the active file. For instance, JPE Inc. maintained a company in the active file from the point a confidentiality agreement was signed until JPE Inc. was no longer interested in the company (or had bought the company). There are usually about fifteen to twenty-five active companies tracked at any one time and perhaps as many as fifty companies that became part of the active file for each company eventually purchased.

Summary of Lead-Flow Generating Process

Although most books on buying a company have a long list of sources for business leads, your best approach is to develop a list of finders or intermediaries who will do your searching for you. To avoid a deluge of leads, you need to be sure you have clarified your acquisition criteria and communicated these criteria to these finders clearly. If you are looking for larger companies, you are more apt to benefit from contacting investment bankers as well. If you pursue the suggestions we have made, it won't take long before you have ten or fifteen finders on your list. It is hard to estimate how many finders you will need. Even a large company such as JPE probably only has about five or ten finders actively sending it leads at any one time, but this is generated from staying in contact, via mailings, e-mails and phone calls, with several hundred brokers and investment bankers over time. Realize however that the active list of ten rotates among the different brokers. Thus, you are wise to maintain contact with everyone on the list unless you have dropped a particular broker for the reasons listed earlier.

If you are getting a steady stream of viable leads that fit your initial criteria, you probably have enough leads. If you are not obtaining enough leads to keep your search active, you may want to review the tips from this section and spend more effort in identifying additional intermediaries.

Chapter Summary

This chapter reviews the primary ways in which you learn about businesses for sale. An elaborate but informal network of brokers is the best direct source of businesses for sale. Although you may be lucky and find your own company by making direct contacts, you are likely to get a much broader lead pool generated with less effort by building your broker network.

This chapter also describes a method for tracking your leads and the typical fee agreement that a buyer-broker (i.e. a broker working for you as the buyer) will ask you to sign.

Exhibit 6.1. An example of a finder's fee agreement

1. This Agreement will be entered into by JPE, Inc., a Michigan corporation (hereinafter "Client"), and _____ (hereinafter "Broker"). The Broker will be responsible for introducing _____ (hereinafter "Company") to the Client with the idea of a possible acquisition by Client. The Client agrees to pay the broker a fee in the manner described in this Agreement.

2. The fee will be based on the value of the transaction entered into. The Client will pay the Broker a fee, payable in cash, upon consummation of any such merger or acquisition transaction with the Company as set forth below.

3. The fee shall be based upon "Total Consideration" in accordance with the following rates: 5% on the first $1,000,000 or "Total Consideration"; plus 4% on the next $1,000,000; plus 3% on the next $1,000,000; plus 2% on the next $1,000,000; plus 1% on the excess over $4,000,000; a minimum fee of $50,000 shall apply.

   "Total Consideration" of the Transaction is defined as the amount of all monies or stock paid for the Company's stock or assets plus the value of any of the Company's interest-bearing debt assumed in connection with the Transaction. In the event that a portion of the "Total Consideration" takes the form of royalties, future considerations payable, licensing agreements, options (excluding there-from any employee stock options), real estate leases, noncompete agreements, consulting agreements, marketing cooperation and similar arrangements, or any other allocation of "Total Consideration" paid or to be paid, the value of these items will be included in the calculation of the commission payable to the Broker. Should a portion of the purchase be a future unidentifiable amount such as an earn-out, royalty, options, etc., they will be included in determining the amount of total fee due the Broker, but will be payable to the Broker upon payment of such amounts, not at the time of closing.

4. If the Client or its controlling stockholders or officers completes a related transaction involving the Company within 18 months from

the date hereof or 12 months from the time negotiations were last terminated, whichever is later, Broker will be compensated under this Agreement, whether or not the Agreement has been terminated.

5. This Agreement may be terminated by either party by providing written notice to the other party. Any termination of the Agreement will not affect Broker's right, if any, to compensation for services rendered under this Agreement.

6. This Agreement shall be construed, governed and enforced in accordance with the laws of the State of Michigan, whose Courts shall have jurisdiction over any dispute arising from the contractual relationships derived from this Agreement. Any controversy or claim arising out of or relating to this Agreement, or the making, performance or interpretation thereof, shall be settled by arbitration in Ann Arbor, Michigan in accordance with the rules of The American Arbitration Association then existing, and judgment on the arbitration award may be entered in any court having jurisdiction over the subject matter of the controversy.

In the unlikely event that arbitration is brought for the enforcement or interpretation of this Agreement, or because of an alleged dispute, breach, default or misrepresentation in connection with any of the provisions of this Agreement, the successful or prevailing party or parties shall be entitled to recover reasonable attorney's fees and other costs incurred in that action or proceeding, in addition to any other relief to which it or they may be entitled.

7. The undersigned acknowledges and agrees that any information provided with respect to the Company is provided by the Company. Broker makes no representations or warranty as to such information. The undersigned further acknowledges sole responsibility to perform a due diligence review prior to any transaction with the Company.

8. The parties recognize that Client has not been provided the name of the Company. If upon disclosure of the identity of the Company, Client can provide written verification that it was previously aware of the Company as an acquisition target, Client and Broker agree that this Agreement will automatically become void and not merely voidable.

ASSIGNMENT DESCRIPTION: _____

ACKNOWLEDGED, ACCEPTED AND AGREED TO:

_____

By: _____   By: _____

     Name: _____   Name: _____

     Title: _____   Title: _____

Dated: _____   Dated: _____

Exhibit 6.2

AN EXAMPLE OF TRACKING THE LEAD SHEET

COMPANY NAME _____   DATE _____
                                   BY _____

LOCATIONS _____   SIZE OF PLANT _____
          _____   _____
          _____   _____
                           _____
OWNERSHIP   _____
INDUSTRY   _____
PRODUCTS   _____
CUSTOMERS   _____

                           19_____   19_____   19_____
ANNUAL SALES - 3 YRS   _____   _____   _____
ANNUAL EBIT   - 3 YRS   _____   _____   _____

TOTAL ASSETS (BV)   _____
BANK DEBT (BV)   _____
EQUITY (BV   _____

KEY MANAGEMENT   _____
NUMBER OF EMPLOYEES   _____
   HOURLY   _____
   SALARIED   _____
   UNION?   _____

ASKING PRICE   _____
PROCESS TIMING   _____
BROKER   _____
SPECIAL COMMENTS   _____

CHAPTER 7

NARROWING YOUR SEARCH: MATCHING BROAD CRITERIA OF YOUR INITIAL BUSINESS PLAN

One of the challenges of buying a company is that the information you need to make a decision is not made available to you all at once. Determining which companies are worth pursuing is a multistage process. Very limited information is provided to the buyer before various legal documents are signed, including a confidentiality agreement, and depending upon the broker, a fee agreement or letter of interest. Even once such documents are signed, significant probing by the buyer is required to get an accurate assessment of a company's value and potential.

Even a carefully designed search process takes eighteen months to two years. The lack of a carefully designed or executed strategy may lead to costly overruns in the acquisition process, a poor purchase choice or no purchase at all.

Initial Criteria for Screening Leads

Before you even contact brokers and establish your lead flow, you should finalize your initial criteria for screening leads. An efficient search depends upon clarifying these criteria in advance and then sticking to them. Useful initial screening criteria include company size (in revenue dollars), profitability, and industry because this information is most likely what a broker will provide before a confidentiality agreement is signed. After you have signed a confidentiality agreement, you are given the company's name and address. At that point, you can screen further using such criteria as location, the reputation or image of the company, and product line. If you are familiar with that industry, you will probably be able to find out whether the company has a clear niche and differentiated product. You may have other criteria over time that are necessary for further consideration, but these are the best criteria to evaluate at the start. Let's review each of these criteria in turn.

Criterion Number One: Company Size

Three key issues relate to the size of company you plan to purchase—your own abilities, your access to capital, and strategic considerations.

Your Own Abilities First, how large a company are you capable of running? The number of employees often dictates the complexity of a business more so than does dollar volume. Especially if you are moving into a different industry, you might be cautioned to consider a company with a similar number of employees or less, rather than base your experience on dollar volume alone. The social dynamics of overseeing a group of eighty or one hundred employees is far different than overseeing a group of twenty or twenty-five employees. You should consider the experience of your management team and the capabilities of managers who plan to stay on with the company you might purchase. But if you plan to be the CEO, be careful not to rely entirely on others. Unless you already have a team assembled, qualified managers are often difficult to find.

Your access to capital A second issue bearing on size relates to the amount of capital you might have available. If you want to be conservative, plan on borrowing roughly 2.5 to 3 times the equity that you can raise. But if you do not expect to raise more than a few hundred thousand dollars in equity, it is foolish to look for a $10-million company. Different industries vary, but in manufacturing, for example, figure that the sales revenues of the company is roughly between 1 and 2 times its price. Thus, if you have about $400,000 in capital, you can seek a company that does between $400,000 and $800,000 in revenues. In distribution, you can probably buy a company for about a third of its sales volume. Find out what the typical ratio is for the industry you are looking at. You don't want to waste time looking at a prospect that you cannot finance or generate expectations for yourself or the seller that are not realistic.

Strategic considerations Finally, in determining size, you need to consider the market and competition. Is market share important in the particular market niche that your company is located in and if so, how does it compare with competitors? The company does not necessarily have to be the largest in its niche, but in some industries, you may not be able to compete well if the company is too small. You need to investigate the industry thoroughly to be able to determine the importance of size for survival, profitability, and growth. You may have to do additional digging to find these answers unless you are already familiar with the industry.

Criterion Number Two: Financial Performance

You should also decide early on in your search how profitable a venture you are seeking. Some buyers intentionally purchase underperforming companies with plans of adding shareholder value by improving the way that they are managed. If this is your strategy, you must make sure that you have the experience and know-how to accomplish this task. The typical company requires seven years or more for a turn-around on average although if you know what to do in an industry, results can be much quicker. J.P. Industries successfully pursued this strategy in the 1980s, building a Fortune 500 company via acquisition and internal growth in about ten years' time.

If you are less experienced or adventuresome, it is very important to seek out a company that is already performing well. There is likely to be some disruption as you take over a business from someone else even if the company has historically performed well.

Information about profitability may be very limited when you first receive a lead from the broker. It may simply say: profitable or not profitable. Once you sign a confidentiality agreement, you should expect to be provided a more detailed financial history of at least three to five years, from which you can evaluate the company's assets and liabilities, its operating margins, net profit, and cash flow.

In reviewing financial information, you need to be equally sensitive to cash flow and profitability. It is quite possible to find a situation where earnings look good because of good accounting practices, but the company doesn't have cash to pay its bills. For instance, sometimes the earnings picture can be improved by stretching out the depreciation over a longer period (and thus lowering the annual expenses). But if you find yourself having to replace equipment before it is fully depreciated then your accounting practices have not fully taken these costs into account and have inflated the earnings picture. It is important in analyzing the financial statements to compare the actual age and life of major capital investments with the depreciation schedule to check for this.

Criterion Number Three: Industry and Product Line

In the 1950s, as the management discipline emerged in business schools and gained respect among business practitioners, the notion held that someone who was a good "manager" in one industry could be a good "manager" in any industry. This might well have been true in the days of domestic competition and weaker competition from the global market, but in today's economy, it is increasingly critical that you know your industry inside out. Very few businesses today can be viewed as "turnkey" operations. To do well, it is essential to understand the nature of the business that you are in and what you need to do to compete in that business. This spans not only the marketing issues of what to sell and what customers will buy but how to operate the business efficiently.

The implications are simple but important: you must select an industry you understand thoroughly. How can you accomplish this? Ideally, you may have worked as an employee for someone else or have had some other direct dealings with that type of company in a professional-support position. Running a manufacturing company is decidedly different than running a company in the service sector or in distribution.

Within the industry, you also need to consider, furthermore, the particular niche that you will be in. Does the company you are considering hold a clear niche or offer a differentiated product, i.e., one that stands out from the crowd? Most small companies do not do well competing head-to-head with large companies with the identical product. But many small companies offer a unique twist that makes them viable. Thus, Proctor and Gamble might be a formidable competitor in soap and detergent products, but many smaller companies do well with a unique scent or content—e.g., organic, hypoallergenic, or other unique formulations not offered by the major companies.

The Confidentiality Agreement

Until you sign a *confidentiality agreement*, you will be fortunate to be able to evaluate even the three criteria—size, profitability, and industry. The confidentiality agreement is a document signed by both the buyer and seller that clarifies how any information emerging from the buying process will be treated. A good confidentiality agreement protects both parties. A number of elements should be included. In particular, a good confidentiality agreement does the following:

Clarifies what is considered confidential information It is often understood, as part of this agreement, that the company being evaluated should mark documents as confidential so that it is clear what is considered confidential and what is not.

States how long the buyer must keep the information confidential Two years is a frequently specified length of time.

Requires the seller to keep the buyer's interest in purchasing the company confidential Especially if the buyer's company is publicly traded, it is important that the seller not divulge the buyer's interest. The Securities and Exchange Commission could make various individuals liable for insider trading violations.

Points out that the confidentiality agreement cannot be construed as a purchase agreement This protects both buyer and seller from misunderstandings.

Clarifies how the information is to be disposed of if the deal is not transacted between the buyer and potential seller A confidentiality agreement needs to provide clear instructions for disposition of materials. Two options can be provided: sending back all information to the target company that were sent by the target company and/or destroying all materials created by the buyer. The latter option is important because as the buyer, you may carry out your own analysis of the target company that you view as somewhat proprietary.

Most brokers have their own form of confidentiality agreement. You should review it carefully. If it doesn't cover all the issues that protect you as the buyer, you should negotiate the terms.

Exhibit 7.1 presents a sample confidentiality agreement.

Information Obtained with the Confidentiality Agreement

Once you have a signed confidentiality agreement, you are likely to receive more information about the company. In the case of the investment banker, you are likely to receive a rather thick book with detailed financials, market, and other information as well as financial forecasts about the company prepared for a fee paid by the seller to the investment bank. Exhibits 7.2 and 7.3 present the table of contents from two memoranda. Although they are different from one another, each generally corresponds to the categories in a typical business plan.

The quality and amount of information you obtain from a buyer-broker varies much more considerably at this point. Rarely if ever will you receive as thorough a book as provided by the investment banker. However, the professional buyer-broker may still provide you with several pages of materials, including more detailed financial statements. The more informal the intermediary, generally, the less the information you will obtain. At the minimum, you would be given the location and name of the business, the owner's name, and a telephone number!

The Fee Agreement

As we discussed in chapter 6, if you are dealing with a buyer-broker, you are likely to be asked to sign a *fee agreement* at about the same time that you sign a confidentiality agreement. The fee agreement is an agreement between the buyer and broker and establishes the fee structure should a sale be consummated based on a lead provided by the broker.

The Letter of Interest

The *letter of interest* is a signed letter by the buyer, which indicates the buyer's interest in purchasing a company within a particular price range. The letter of interest is almost exclusively used by investment bankers to screen prospective buyers for the seller. The purpose of the letter of interest is to provide the investment banker or other brokers representing the sellers' interest with information to whittle down and eliminate unqualified buyers.

The major goal of the letter of interest from the buyer's standpoint is to "make the cut." The investment banker typically does not want to bring lots of people into the company. In particular, he or she wants to weed out the "tire kickers." If your offering price is too low or the seller has other reasons for not wanting to consider your offer, you can be excluded from any further consideration of purchasing the company. The investment banker will often choose only about a half-dozen companies (three to ten being the outside range) to be considered as possible buyers past this point.

Exhibit 7.4 presents a sample letter of interest. The elements in a well-constructed letter of interest presents an offering price range, clarifies that the letter of interest is not to be construed as a purchase agreement, includes a confidentiality clause, makes reference to financing plans, and in the case of a buyer whose company is publicly held, should state the restrictions on stock purchase for those knowledgeable of the pending deal. Let's look at each of these issues a little more closely.

Presentation of an offering price range The most important function of this letter is to indicate an upper and lower limit that the buyer is likely to pay for the seller's company. It is in no way binding on the buyer, but it is a critical step in the deal-making process.

If your offering price range is too low, but the seller might still have an interest in you as a buyer, the investment banker may call you to say that you sound interesting, but you're 25% below almost everybody else. They might ask if you really want to look at this company. A good way to respond, in such a case, is to say, "If there's information I don't have, I might consider the company at this (higher) price." In such a case, you might still be considered as a buyer. This is more likely if you send other background material along with the letter of interest so that the seller knows more about you.

Clarification that the letter of interest is not an offer or binding commitment on the part of the buyer This is similar to the statement in the confidentiality agreement and is included to protect both buyer and seller.

A confidentiality clause A confidentiality clause should be included that protects the buyer. It should state that the letter's contents, including the offering price, not be disclosed to anyone other than the company's board of directors and authorized representatives in the divesture.

Financing of the deal The letter of interest might note that the buyer is able to finance the deal and who might help in financing the deal. This helps to establish your financial credibility. Alternatively, as in the sample letter of interest, it might simply indicate that the transaction is subject to the buyer's ability to obtain financing.

Restriction of stock purchase of the buyer's company In the case of a buyer that is publicly traded, the letter of interest also cautions the members of the company up for sale that United States securities laws restrict persons with nonpublic information from purchasing or selling securities of the buyer.

Early Proceeding When a Letter of Interest is not Asked for

You might wonder what happens when a letter of interest is not requested, a situation that is more likely to occur when a buyer-broker serves as intermediary. You don't always send a letter of interest because it might not be necessary. Although you might indicate your interest in some point in a letter, many of the issues are often dealt with orally in direct contact with the seller. Your expression of interest is usually done orally in face-to-face contact with the owner.

For instance, during the early stages of one acquisition, Psarouthakis visited the company and carried out several meetings and discussion between his staff and the company owners. At a certain point, they discussed price in general terms. There might have been an unofficial letter that indicated interest, but in principle, the negotiations bypassed the letter of interest and proceeded orally until the letter of intent was worked out.

Reviewing the Initial Documents

Based on the documentation that you receive, once you receive the confidentiality agreement, you may learn enough about the condition and location of the business to decide whether or not to pursue it further. You might find, for instance, that even though the company is profitable, it is already too highly leveraged to withstand the type of buyout you had in mind. Or you might learn that much of its business is geared toward providing parts for a model that will be discontinued in the near future. Perhaps the location is undesirable, based on your personal preferences. These issues and others might lead you to decide it is not even worth the expense and time of paying a visit to the company headquarters to meet the seller. Historically, at JPE Inc., about half of the leads for which confidentiality agreements had been signed were dropped at this point. The other half were pursued with a site visit and preliminary due diligence, which will be discussed in the next chapter.

Chapter Summary

The first "filters" for your leads are the initial criteria that you set in your acquisition plan. Although you will have many more issues to review as information unfolds, it is unpractical to consider much more than the total sales revenues, degree of profitability, and industry at the start because this is all the information you are likely to get from most brokers or other sources before having to sign a confidentiality agreement.

Once you sign a confidentiality agreement, you are wise to set up more detailed criteria. Some of the more common criteria used at this next stage include the location, product line, the reputation of the company—if easily determined, growth patterns for the industry and the company up for sale, more detail about profitability, cash flow, and liquidity, and of course, the overall appeal of the business to you, personally.

The fee agreement is usually also required at about the same time as the confidentiality agreement when you are dealing with a buyer-broker. The broker wants to be assured that he or she will get a commission if the sale goes through. This is not needed in a case where the broker represents the seller, as in the case of the investment banker. However, in the latter situation, once you have signed a confidentiality agreement and received extensive written material, you will be asked, within a few weeks, typically, to send a letter of interest, indicating the range of value that you place on the company. Only a handful of prospective buyers are then allowed to continue considering the company for purchase, including an initial company visit and subsequent due diligence.

It is not unusual to sign a confidentiality agreement for approximately fifty companies for every company you actually buy. Of course, this does not happen all at once. This is a cumulative total over the course of an eighteen-month to two-year search.

Once you sign a confidentiality agreement and receive additional information, you can probably eliminate all but a few from further evaluation. Or in the case of the investment banker, some of these may be eliminated for you. For the remaining few, you are ready to proceed to the initial site visit and preliminary due diligence.

Exhibit 7.1. An example of a short form of a confidentiality agreement

In connection with Buyer's (Buyer") evaluation of _____ (the "Company") as a possible acquisition candidate, Buyer has requested the right to review certain nonpublic information regarding the Company. In consideration of disclosure of such information (the "Information") and Buyer's evaluation thereof, the parties agree as follows:

1. The information will be used by Buyer solely for the purpose of evaluation a possible transaction with the Company, and for a period of two years from the date thereof, the Information will be kept confidential by Buyer and its directors, officers, employees and advisors ("Buyer Representatives"). Such information shall be disclosed only to those Buyer Representatives who have a need to know the Information for the purpose of evaluating a possible transaction with the Company.

2. "Information" shall not include any information, which (i) at the time of disclosure or thereafter is generally known by the public (other than as a result of its disclosure by Buyer or Buyer Representatives) or (ii) was or becomes available to Buyer on a non-confidential basis from a person not otherwise bound by a confidentiality agreement with the Company or is not otherwise prohibited from transmitting the information to Buyer.

3. The Company and its representatives hereby acknowledge that they are aware that the United States securities laws prohibit any person who has material nonpublic information concerning the matters, which are the subject of this Agreement from purchasing or selling securities of Buyer (and options, warrants and rights relating thereto) and from communicating such information to any person under circumstances in which it is reasonably foreseeable that such person is likely to purchase or sell such securities.

4. The parties hereto agree that unless and until a definitive agreement between Buyer and the Company with respect to any transaction has been executed and delivered, neither Buyer nor the Company will be under any legal obligation of any kind

whatsoever with respect to such transaction by virtue of (i) this Agreement or (ii) any written or oral expression with respect to such a transaction by Buyer or Company Representatives except for the matters agreed to herein.

5. If Buyer decides not to proceed with an acquisition of the Company or upon request by the Company, Buyer will return the Information to the Company, or destroy the Information at the Company's request.

If you are in agreement with the foregoing, please execute and return one copy of this Agreement to Buyer.

Buyer, Inc [Company]
By: _____   By: _____
    Title: _____   Title: _____
Address: _____   Address: _____

Exhibit 7.2. Sample table of contents from memoranda provided by investment bankers

I. EXECUTIVE SUMMARY ....
The Company ....
Reason for Sale ....
Summary Operating Performance ....
Investment Considerations ....

II. INDUSTRY ....
General ....
Trends Affecting Automotive Suppliers ....

III. BUSINESS ....
History ....
Strategy ....
Products ....
Customers ....
Competition ....
New Product Development ....
Sales and Marketing ....
Production ....
Manufacturing ....
Facilities ....
Capacity ....
Systems ....
Quality Control ....
Management ....
Employees ....
Contingent Liabilities ....

IV. HISTORICAL FINANCIAL REVIEW ....
Income Statements ....
Balance Sheets ....
Capital Expenditures ....

V. PROJECTED FINANCIAL REVIEW ....
Introduction ....

INDEX OF CHARTS

Exhibit 7.2a. Another sample table of contents from memoranda provided by investment bankers

EXECUTIVE SUMMARY

BUSINESS DESCRIPTION

MANAGEMENT AND EMPLOYEES

FINANCIAL DATA

OFFERING PROCEDURES

APPENDICES

I. AUDITED FINANCIAL STATEMENTS FOR THE YEARS ENDED DECEMBER 31, 20x1 AND 20x2

II. AUDITED FINANCIAL STATEMENTS FOR THE YEARS ENDED DECEMBER 31, 20x0 AND 20x1

III. CORPORATE BROCHURE

Exhibit 7.3. Short-form letter of interest

[Date]

Dear [Target]:

We have reviewed the information you have provided us regarding _____ (the "Company") and would like to submit our proposal under which _____ ("Buyer") would be willing to proceed with an evaluation of the Company for the possible acquisition by Buyer of substantially all of the assets of the Company.

Our preliminary assessment of the value of the Company is in the range $_____ to $_____ plus the assumption of accounts payable and accrued liabilities. This value is based upon information you provided, including the _____, 20xx balance sheet.

The transaction would be subject to Buyer obtaining either debt or equity financing in an amount and upon terms and conditions satisfactory to Buyer.

This letter is intended to be an indication of our interest and is not an offer or binding commitment on the part of Buyer. The terms of this letter of interest are confidential and should not be disclosed to anyone other than the Company Board of Directors and authorized representatives involved in the divestiture. The Company, including its officers, directors, shareholders and representatives, are hereby advised that Buyer is a publicly traded company and that the United States securities laws restrict persons with material nonpublic information about a company obtained directly or indirectly from that company from purchasing or selling securities of such company, or from communicating such information to any other person under circumstances in which it is reasonably foreseeable that such person is likely to purchase or sell such securities.

We look forward to moving on to the next step of the process and learning more about the Company. We would be glad to schedule due diligence activities as soon as is practical for both parties. If you have any questions regarding the content of this letter, please give me a call.

Very truly yours,

Buyer

CHAPTER 8

THE EVALUATION PROCESS:
AN OVERVIEW

Evaluation of the business deal is an ongoing process that begins the moment you obtain a lead from a broker and continues through closing of the deal. Valuing a business could become the most challenging component of the acquisition process, principally, because it is more of an art than science. The acquirer should remember that the value of the business to him is not the price that he/she should pay. Furthermore, the acquirer should be keenly aware as he negotiates the price that the seller has, usually, a strong emotional attachment to the business he built and therefore he/she believes subjectively that his business has higher value/price than it really does. The challenge for the buyer is to develop a price based as much as possible on objective considerations and facts and then tactfully but clearly present them to the seller during the negotiation process.

Think of the evaluation process as a filtering process of your flow of leads through successive screens as you obtain more information about each lead until you have narrowed your leads down to one final choice.

Based on actions you take, there are typically five discrete stages of information acquisition that will help you in narrowing down your leads. As you obtain more information, you are able to filter or screen out those leads that are less likely to meet your criteria and provide you with the results you desire. These stages or filters are as follows:

Filter 1:   Initial information provided by your broker (Filters initial lead pool from hundreds or thousands to about 50 leads)

Filter 2:   Initial data from the broker after a confidentiality agreement is signed (allows you to weed out all but about 25-30 leads, approximately speaking)

Filter 3:   Information obtained from visit to the company and preliminary due diligence (provides you with means to reduce lead pool further to about a dozen target companies)

Filter 4:   Response to your letter of intent by the seller (provides you with means to reduce leads further to about 3-5 target companies)

Filter 5:   Results of formal due diligence and final negotiations for the purchase agreement (narrows your search from several down to the one company you actually buy).

Filter 1: Initial Information Provided by Your Broker

When you first obtain a lead from a broker, the information is likely to be limited to total revenues, profitability of the company, and possibly, the industry, and some product information. Sometimes you will not even obtain this much information.

If you have followed the suggestions we have provided you about lead flow, you will eventually receive hundreds, if not thousands of leads. At this stage, you will be lucky to have sufficient information to compare against your initial acquisition criteria. Most leads can be quickly weeded out because they are either much too large or small, are in the wrong industry, or do not meet your profitability criteria, or perhaps, are in the wrong region. You won't collect these leads all at one time, but in the course of a year or two, it is quite possible that you will screen this many leads, especially if you include the books of leads that some organizations might send to you.

You may be tempted to investigate leads that don't fit your broad criteria. Try to resist this temptation. If a lead does not match your size, profitability, and industry criteria, you should reply quickly to the broker sending you a lead so that he or she can send it on to a more appropriate buyer. Sticking to your criteria will help you to respond quickly to brokers, and in turn, keep your network active. And you don't have the time to pursue every prospect in detail.

Handling Situations with Incomplete Information

What do you do if you have incomplete information on a lead—such as a lack of industry information?

If the lead interests you, try to obtain whatever information the broker is willing to extend to you. However, the broker is likely to ask you to sign a confidentiality agreement and in the case of a buyer-broker, a fee agreement, before you are given much more information to go on. Signing a confidentiality agreement is typically the next step in obtaining more detailed information about companies for which you have an interest. You may sign a confidentiality agreement for as many as fifty leads over time, if you stick to your initial criteria.

In sum, until you have enough information to reject a lead, i.e., when it doesn't match your initial criteria, don't ignore it. The lead could turn out to be the company best suited to your criteria, and then you know to pursue the lead. Even if you don't know the broker, you may want to pursue it anyway but reject his or her offer the next time you pursue a lead if the company proved a waste of your time.

Filter 2: Initial Data from the Broker
After a Confidentiality Agreement has been Signed

The second key filter is after the confidentiality agreement is signed and returned to the broker. The amount of information you are going to receive once you sign a confidentiality agreement depends upon the sophistication and type of broker you are working with. You may expect to

John Psarouthakis and Lorraine Uhlaner

receive a rather thick binder or "book" where the broker is an investment banker working for the seller. You may receive only a few pages of additional information and a financial report from a professional broker, possibly even less from the informal intermediary. The most informal intermediaries may simply provide you with the seller's address and phone number and suggest that you call to set up a meeting.

Based on the additional information you receive at this point, you should be able to narrow your active leads even further, typically by as much as 50%. Thus, assuming that you sign approximately fifty confidentiality agreements over a two-year period, you may eliminate twenty-five or thirty companies on the basis of the materials you are provided by the broker once you sign the confidentiality agreement. For instance, you may judge that the company size, profitability, industry, specific product or service, or location is inappropriate to your needs.

The Letter of Interest: The Ticket to a Company Visit

An investment banker is likely to send much more detailed information at this stage than a buyer-broker is likely to send. You will be asked for a letter of interest upon receipt of a book or binder of information about the company before you are allowed to visit the company and meet with the seller. The letter of interest must state a price you estimate that you are willing to pay for the company. Although the price you propose is not legally binding, it is the key criterion for determining whether you are chosen to visit the company as a prospective buyer. You are advised to consult an attorney before signing the letter of interest.

Filter 3: Information Obtained from Visit to the Company and Preliminary Due Diligence

Data collected in the preliminary due diligence is the next filter in the evaluation process. For the few dozen companies that you find particularly attractive, based on the initial information provided by the broker, it is helpful to carry out preliminary due diligence and to meet the seller before proceeding to formal due diligence.

Why Conduct a Preliminary Due Diligence?

The distinction between preliminary and formal due diligence is an essential aspect of the efficient evaluation process. During preliminary due diligence, your goal is to obtain enough information on a *low-cost* basis about the company to determine whether or not it is worth carrying out formal due diligence. To keep costs down, *and* to increase your opportunities for direct contact with the seller, preliminary due diligence should be conducted by yourself and your management team. If you come across information in preliminary due diligence that clearly rules out this prospect, you have saved a lot of needless expense during the formal due diligence process. Furthermore, the rapport that you build with the seller during a properly executed preliminary due diligence process may surface information that even the most exhaustive analysis of documentation may fail to uncover.

Failure by the seller to reveal important information may lead to renegotiation of the price or even a cancellation of the purchase agreement but rarely provides reimbursement to the buyer of the expense of formal due diligence. A business acquaintance recently purchased a company in England in an arrangement where ownership was transferred with no money down. The arrangement seemed almost too good to be true, and it was. The day after closing, the new owners discovered a drawer full of unpaid bills that the previous owner had failed to disclose, in essence, bankrupting the firm. Although the new owners were able to get out of the deal, they are still out $50,000 in legal and due diligence expenses for evaluating the company and negotiating the closing and even more, if one considers the time lost and other business opportunities missed in the process. The experience also underscores the need for direct contact with the owner. If a situation seems too good to be true, follow your intuition and pursue the situation personally until you have all the answers. Trust your own instincts. In the Bristish company mentioned earlier, a well-respected consulting firm that performed the formal due diligence missed any cues that trouble was brewing.

Questions to Ask During Preliminary Due Diligence

You will want to be particularly attentive to the following key aspects at this stage:

1. Why is the seller selling his or her business?
2. What is the overall financial condition of the company?
3. Is the company in an acceptable and desirable location to meet your personal and company needs and to be successful?
4. Is the seller likely to sell within a price range that you are willing to pay? (In the case of the investment banker, presumably if you have been selected based on your letter of interest, you have already determined this.)
5. Has the company been kept up pretty well, or is it run down to the point it would be difficult to make successful?
6. Are there any glaring problems at this stage—environmental, legal suits, etc., that might make it undesirable to buy this business?

You will probably come up with your own additional questions, but you should be able to gather information to move you toward an approximate answer to these questions before investing in costly consultants to review documents in more detail.

Depending once again on the nature of the broker handling the deal, the amount of information you are likely to have prior to your first visit to the prospective company will vary enormously. In either event, you will want to arrange a visit directly with the seller as early in the evaluation process as possible. At this point, you should already have determined that the company meets your initial criteria and is also located in a suitable location for your needs.

You need to find out why the seller is selling as early in the process as possible. Some sellers are prodded into showing their company by an insistent broker but are not very motivated to sell except perhaps at an unreasonably high price. Or you may have a seller motivated by the wrong reasons. Perhaps business has not been handled well in recent months or years and has deteriorated to the point it would be a bad purchase at any price. In a case where the company has developed a bad reputation among customers, this is particularly difficult to correct. Assuming that the company meets the initial criteria laid out in your acquisition plan, you have identified a serious seller, and the company has a good reputation, then you are likely to proceed to formal due diligence.

Filter 4: Information Gathered from Formal Due Diligence

Due to the high cost of formal due diligence, it is very important that you sign a letter of intent and negotiate an *exclusivity clause* before proceeding. The exclusivity clause in the letter of intent is supposed to prevent the seller from selling to another buyer during the period that you conduct formal due diligence. Without such a clause negotiated and signed by both buyer and seller, you may invest several thousands of dollars evaluating a company only to lose the deal to another buyer.

If you have been thorough at the preliminary due diligence stage, you are likely to submit a letter of intent for about a dozen of the twenty-five or thirty of the active leads for which you performed preliminary due diligence—again estimating roughly over a two-year period. However, since not all letters of intent are accepted by the seller, anticipate that only about three to five of these are actually worked out and signed by both seller and buyer. For this small subgroup of leads, you are finally ready to proceed with formal due diligence.

Formal due diligence involves a thorough investigation of all aspects of the business: legal, marketing, financial, environmental, and managerial. Formal due diligence is the most costly part of the deal-making process. Do not be in too big a rush to proceed to this stage, or you could waste a lot of valuable money and time. Worse, you might use up the initial investment that you had set aside for due diligence on the wrong companies.

Filter 5: Final Selection of the Company

Although, again, each deal is unique, it is typical to complete some level of formal due diligence for four or five companies to every one that you actually close. At any point in the evaluation process, even during formal due diligence, you might uncover problems or issues with the company that make it undesirable for you to purchase. These problems might relate to environmental pollution, a pending product liability lawsuit, or perhaps falsified financial records that inflated the company's performance. It is never too late to back out of a deal, prior to closing, although once you sign a letter of intent, you may have to pay a penalty if you back out of the deal. However, this is far better than purchasing a company that will not work out for you.

Even seasoned executives often get too absorbed in the deal at this point to look at it objectively. Psychologists refer to this phenomenon as *escalating commitment*. To avoid this trap, you must start with sufficient capital to carry out formal due diligence several times, if needed. Otherwise, you are more likely to feel you are, running out of time and money and must go through with a questionable deal. Keeping your lead flow going until a deal actually closes also reduces the urge to close on the wrong deal.

Chapter Summary

In sum, the evaluation process takes place in successive stages or filters as you progress more deeply into the deal. At any point along the way that you feel uncomfortable with the deal, you should not go through with it. However, be aware that even in deals that go through, extensive problem-solving is often required in order to complete the deal. The filters are as follows:

Filter 1:   Initial information provided by your broker (Filters initial lead pool from hundreds or thousands to about 50 leads)

Filter 2:   Initial data from the broker after a confidentiality agreement is signed (allows you to weed out all but about 25-30 leads, approximately speaking)

Filter 3:   Information obtained from the visit to the company and preliminary due diligence (provides you with means to reduce lead pool further to about a dozen target companies)

Filter 4:   Response to your letter of intent by the seller (provides you with means to reduce leads further to about 3-5 target companies)

Filter 5:   Results of formal due diligence and final negotiations for the purchase agreement (narrows your search from several down to the one company you actually buy.)

As each lead comes through, it is subjected to these different filters. A lead may drop out at any stage in the screening process, with only one making it all the way to the end of the search. However, you should keep your lead flow going and continue to screen new leads until you have actually closed the deal. The evaluation process may turn up information at any stage that deters you from making the sale, and you are far more likely to resist a bad purchase if you have other deals in the pipeline. An understanding of this process is also helpful in budgeting the amount of money you will need in your search. Ideally, you want to have ample funds to visit a few dozen companies and to carry out formal due diligence on at least three or four companies before finalizing the deal. Of course, you may get lucky and find a company with less effort, but that is the exception rather than the rule.

CHAPTER 9

PRELIMINARY DUE DILIGENCE

An extremely important and usually the most critical part of the acquisition process is a well-conducted due diligence. This is a stage where not only the financial condition of the company is thoroughly checked out—far from it. You check out the entire business—its operations, supplier relations, customer relations, employee relations, relations with the financial institutions it deals with, its strategy, business development plans, and more, as we will see in this and the next chapter.

It is rather evident that this process can be a very expensive undertaking. Therefore, it is strongly recommended that the due diligence process is divided in to two stages: the preliminary stage and the formal stage. Basically your goal in preliminary due diligence, once you have obtained enough information to have an understanding that the company meets your criteria, is to determine early in the process whether or not there are any obvious skeletons in the closet—anything of significance hidden from you that could seriously jeopardize the value of the company, whether there is a drop in sales or unanticipated major expenses, any major lawsuits and the like.

This process continues, only with more detail, in the formal due diligence phase once the letter of intent is signed. Not all explanations of the buying process make the distinction between preliminary and formal due diligence. However, this distinction is essential to carrying out an efficient, affordable yet effective search.

Formal due diligence is very expensive, if done correctly, costing anywhere between $50,000 for a very small company to $100,000 or more, depending upon the size and complexity of the company. You will quickly run out of money in your search without very carefully prescreening the companies for which you plan to conduct a formal due diligence, even though a lead may meet your broad criteria. Thus, you want to find out as much about a company as you can, as inexpensively as you can, before you commit to a formal due diligence process.

By contrast, preliminary due diligence primarily costs you your time and travel expenses. You may also need some legal or accounting assistance, depending upon your own background, but it is still far less costly than when you enter into formal due diligence. By separating preliminary from formal due diligence, you are basically separating out the issues that you can find out about relatively cheaply and quickly from those that may require extensive investigation and the aid of costly consulting services. JPE Inc. estimated that it spent an average of only a few thousand dollars in exploring each lead during preliminary due diligence, relying primarily on its own salaried employees for legal and accounting in-house.

Typically, you can expect to narrow down your lead pool from about twenty-five or thirty to about eight or ten companies over a two-year period that pass the screen of the preliminary due diligence filter, and for which you actually prepare a letter of intent. Of those, you still might only carry out formal due diligence for four or five companies or perhaps even fewer until you find the correct company to buy if you follow the procedures outlined here.

This chapter reviews the third stage of the filtering process of your lead flow that we refer to as *preliminary due diligence.*

Definition of Due Diligence

Due diligence is the careful, thorough evaluation of a company that you carry out to properly assess its value to you and also to uncover any potentially damaging issues that may cost you money after the sale is closed. Quite literally, due diligence is the care and caution in investigating the seller's company. If you are a publicly held company, due diligence has legal implications. You are expected to investigate certain aspects of a purchase before spending shareholder money to close the deal. But well beyond the legal requirements and even if all the money you are spending is your own, it is critical that you evaluate a company thoroughly before buying it.

Because of its high expense, conducting a formal due diligence for more than a few companies in your search becomes highly impractical. *Preliminary due diligence* is simply the first step in due diligence, which you can carry out relatively affordably and primarily with your own efforts before you investigate the company in such exhaustive detail. You should define your own plan for preliminary due diligence so that you can keep the overall costs of the sale to a reasonable level. Select among the evaluation criteria those that you or any salaried personnel can do initially yourselves before hiring expensive outside consultants.

When Preliminary Due Diligence Occurs

The timing of preliminary due diligence is slightly different depending upon the broker involved in the sale. In the case of the deal represented by the investment banker, preliminary due diligence refers to the evaluation of the company that takes place after the letter of interest is accepted and before the letter of intent is signed.

In the case of the deal represented by buyer-brokers, both the professional broker and intermediary, you are not likely to sign a letter of interest. Thus, the onset of preliminary due diligence is a little less precise. But generally speaking, it is the investigation you carry out after having signed the confidentiality agreement, the receiving of initial information, and the decision to pursue the lead before you sign a letter of intent.

The letter of intent is an important milestone ending the preliminary due diligence. Once the letter of intent is signed, you are often committed to carry out formal due diligence and to close the deal within a set time frame and/or to pay a break-up fee if you decide not to go through with the deal. At the same time, until you sign a letter of intent, you are not protected should the seller decide to sell the company to someone else. Thus, by its very nature, preliminary due diligence needs to be low cost because you lack exclusivity protection during this period, i.e., the seller can always go with another buyer.

The Goals of Preliminary Due Diligence

Ideally, you want to accomplish the following key goals of the preliminary due diligence:

1. To determine whether the seller is really serious about selling the company and if so, why does he or she want to sell it
2. To determine whether this is the company that you want to buy
3. To determine the price you want to offer to the seller for the company in your letter of intent
4. To develop rapport with the seller and
5. To uncover any red flags that suggest you should abandon this lead.

Goal 1: To determine whether the seller is really serious about selling the company and if so, why does he or she want to sell it In the case of the seller represented by an investment banker, you can assume that the seller is serious about selling. He or she has typically already spent a part of the fee to the investment banker for the preparation of the memorandum or book that you receive once you sign a confidentiality agreement. However, in the case of more informal intermediaries, you might run into the seller that has been goaded into meeting with you by a convincing broker and agrees to do so primarily out of idle curiosity. You probably want to weed out such cases because these are the leads most likely to go sour during the long negotiation process and may turn out to be the most expensive deals.

You should also determine the seller's motive for selling. A thorough understanding of the seller's motive may lead your due diligence in certain directions that you might not have thought about otherwise.

Goal 2: To determine whether this is the company that you want to buy The second goal of preliminary due diligence is a further assessment of the fit of this company to your original business plan. Obviously, if you run into damaging information during the formal due diligence phase, you might still decide not to buy a company, but you need to sort out overall fit with your criteria and goals at this stage, before you spend a lot of money on formal due diligence. You might still go forward with the deal if this company matches your requirements for size, location, type of product or service, growth rate, profitability, core capabilities, or whatever other criteria you have set up for yourself. But you will want to guard against potential problems by negotiating a price and escrow arrangements in keeping with the perceived risks. If this company does not match very well with your original acquisition plan, review carefully whether or not you are really interested in this type of company or if you are being pushed forward by the momentum of the lead process. Even if this company is the type of company you want, is this *particular* company the right one for you? Is this a company that has created a successful market niche for itself?

Goal 3: To determine the price that you want to offer to the seller for the company in your letter of intent Another objective of the preliminary due diligence phase is to determine the purchase price as closely as possible, barring unknown contingencies that might affect the value of the company, which you might still uncover before closing. The price stated in the letter of intent, although still nonbinding, should be as accurate as possible so that you are sure the seller and you are not too far apart in final negotiations. Otherwise, you risk the deal going sour after having spent significant time and dollars during the formal due diligence phase.

Of course, before formal due diligence is completed, you cannot know all the contingencies that might affect the final price. But these unknown costs can be covered by contingency clauses in the letter of intent that must be resolved in the formal due diligence process prior to closing.

Goal 4: To develop rapport with the seller Building rapport with the seller is another very important goal of the preliminary due diligence process. A seller is not obligated to sell to a particular buyer. The highest bid does not automatically get the deal. Many a deal has been made or lost based on the chemistry between buyer and seller. Chemistry becomes even more important when the seller is needed to stay on to help manage the company and/or is helping to finance the deal in some way. Rapport is important where multiple bidding is involved, as in the case of investment bankers. It can also be a key factor in the purchase of the family business, where the owner feels a sense of duty and responsibility to longtime employees who may stay on with the business after it changes to new ownership.

Goal 5: To uncover any red flags that suggest you should abandon this lead At any stage of due diligence, you want to uncover potentially damaging problems. But red flags ascertained during the preliminary due diligence phase could save you the expense of formal due diligence and/or a break-up fee if you decide the problem is serious enough to abandon the deal. A special section later in this chapter examines these red flags in more detail.

Conducting Preliminary Due Diligence

Preliminary due diligence has three aspects: the company visit, a preliminary review of documents, and a meeting with the seller. Again, the pattern is somewhat different depending upon the size of company, and in particular, whether or not an investment banker is involved.

The Company Visit

The company visit is a very important aspect of preliminary due diligence. Ideally, you want to make two company visits and to arrange at least part of that time to meet alone with the seller, both to build rapport and to develop your intuitive sense about the company and its owner. Be prepared to stay about four to six hours for each visit. Don't be disappointed if you are scheduled for a shorter visit, especially if an investment banker is involved. But be prepared to stay longer if the owner is interested. This is an ideal time to get to know the seller, both to build rapport and to learn his or her motives for selling the company.

The first company visit varies in timing, content, and purpose, depending upon the broker involved with the deal. Let's take the case, first, of the investment-banker-represented deal. If your letter of interest is accepted, you will be formally scheduled for a visit, at which time managers from the seller's company make a formal presentation. You will probably meet with several managers of the company in a conference room. They will provide an overview of the company that often follows the content of the memorandum quite closely. For instance, they may describe their market and its growth potential, their manufacturing processes and how they are improving them, their financial condition, and other basic information about the organization. Quite often, the investment banker has assisted in preparing the presentation so it is quite polished. Following the presentation, the buyer has the opportunity to ask questions then to take a plant tour and afterward to return to the conference room for additional discussion.

Even if the investment banker generally stays fairly close by the seller during this visit, you will find it helpful to try to steal as many moments alone with the seller as you can, in order to begin developing some rapport with him or her. Personal contact time with the seller is very useful because it develops your intuitive or physical sensing of the seller—how trustworthy he or she is and whether or not he is telling the truth. You can also be more persuasive in face-to-face contact than you could in a letter to the seller. Face-to-face contact is simply a richer medium for information than written documentation. For adequate face-to-face contact to occur, you often have to arrange for a second company visit. A second visit also indicates your strong interest, which may be beneficial in a situation where you are competing with other buyers.

In other settings where the investment banker is not involved, the first visit is likely to be much less formal. When the investment banker is not involved, you may simply chat with the owner in his office and take a tour of the plant.

Regardless of the type of broker involved, you want to try to have the opportunity to share your background as well so that the owner begins to gain confidence in you as the buyer. This is a very important aspect of the procedure followed at JPE Inc.

Review of Documentation During the Preliminary Due Diligence Phase

You begin review of company documentation during the preliminary due diligence phase.

Review of documentation when an investment banker is involved Review of documentation during the preliminary due diligence is likely to be much more formalized where an investment banker is involved. In that instance, either at the first company visit or within the following few weeks, the seller will have prepared a due diligence room where they keep all the paperwork they think you might be interested in. Remember at this stage, there are still five or six other prospective buyers. You are not going to be allowed to speak with suppliers, customers, or employees other than a few key managers. Thus, most of your information will be culled from the company visit, the documentation, and your general knowledge of the industry. (For instance, if you are a competitor, supplier, or customer for the same industry, you may already know what the customers think of this company.)

The documentation is likely to be wide-ranging including financial statements, benefits package information, including health or pension funds, reports they have done on environmental work, internal revenue service records, and basically, anything else you find in paperwork form. Sometimes the investment banker would like you to do more work at this stage in the proceedings than is really necessary. Remember that sifting through thousands of pages of documentation is costly, especially if you need outside help. But you do want to peruse the documentation sufficiently so that you are satisfied that there are no serious red flags you can spot right away.

Review of documentation when a buyer-broker is involved Preliminary due diligence, especially this aspect, is much more difficult when the buyer-broker is involved because there is no book or memorandum prepared. Nor is there likely to be a due diligence room set up with all the documentation in one place. No one has gathered the information, and you are likely to need at least three people involved—an accountant, a lawyer, and a financial auditor to help with the preliminary due diligence to assist with determining the appropriate price and to draft the letter of intent. Typically at the preliminary due diligence phase, even when an informal intermediary is involved, you will want to ask for a variety of readily available documents. You usually want to ask for union contracts, any benefits documentation, group medical health, pension plans, or any documents related to other employee related regulation, such as in the US, for instance, the American Disabilities Act, or 401 (k) plans. You should also ask for copies of any government environmental agency studies that may have been done. You will also want financial information for the past several years as well as any available projections. You may only scan much of the material at this stage, but it is helpful to begin to gather and review this material anyway.

Meeting with the Seller

You may be able to meet with the seller as a part of your first company visit. If not, it is important to try to set up some time when you can meet alone with the seller. Although when an investment banker is involved, you may have to be persuasive about this. There are a few key reasons you need to meet with the seller early on. First of all, as mentioned earlier, you want to know whether he is a willing and serious seller. You don't want to waste a lot of time if he's not really planning to sell. Secondly, if he or she is serious, what is the price that he or she has in mind? Sometimes you can come right out and ask the investment banker. They won't tell you directly, but they will often tell you the high side of the range. Or the seller may tell you. Thirdly, if the seller is willing, you want to determine whether you are dealing with a reasonable person. You may have to follow your intuition on this one although it is a good sign if he has professional advisors. Fourth, does the seller have partners, and if so, are they influential in the sale? You don't want to waste your time convincing one partner to sell only to find out that other partners have been excluded from important conversation. If partners are not actively participating in the discussion, will they rely on his decision? You may want to try to verify this independently if you can. Finally, you want to find out why the seller wants to sell. If it is to settle an estate, or he is getting older and plans to retire, then these are pretty good reasons.

One of the red flags to watch for at this stage is whether or not the owner has lost his or her competitive edge. One sign of this might be that they talk a lot about competition, in the manner that it is almost a fixation. Another is how recently they have been involved with development of new product. This is a problem because companies can fall quickly behind their competitors when led by such an owner and may have a difficult time catching up. He may have stopped managing the company for the future. A second red flag is that the seller is strictly motivated by price alone (and won't sell unless the price is high enough). These are situations, as mentioned earlier, where the seller may not be motivated enough to complete the sale.

Type of Information You Are Likely to Collect During Preliminary Due Diligence

This section highlights some of the issues you are most likely to investigate at the preliminary due diligence phase. Some of the issues include the financial condition of the company, marketing data including sales trends, the union contract, benefits, manufacturing processes, and any environmental issues.

Financial condition You want to examine the overall profitability of the firm and whether expenses are properly accounted for on the income statement, rather than being counted as assets. You want to examine the size of inventory in relationship to overall assets, the cash flow of the company, sales trends, and overall debt. It is very hard to acquire a company that is already highly leveraged especially if you plan to borrow significantly to buy the company.

Marketing data You want to examine the viability of the product or service, first and foremost. If sales have been flat or downward in recent years, you need to explore the cause of such trends. But you also need to examine future trends. For instance, does the company rely too heavily on any one customer, on a product that will become rapidly obsolete, or is it about to lose a major customer? Is the company bringing new products on line in a timely fashion? You may be able to determine some of these issues quickly from the financial data and your knowledge of the industry. Others may have to wait until formal due diligence.

Union contract and benefits You may not want to inherent a company contract that promises costly benefits. You must also weigh the timing of buying the company if a major contract is up for renegotiation shortly after you are likely to close on the deal. It is a very difficult situation to face. You might want to see if the medical plan is transferable when ownership changes. In the union contract, in particular, you might want to examine whether employees are flexible in their job assignments, especially in a manufacturing setting. Basically, you look for issues that might cause you to lose interest or hedge on the price.

Some red flags to look for in this area may be that the pay is too high, that there are too many classifications, or that the contract is up for negotiation pretty quickly. It is helpful to get to know your employees and union before you need to negotiate a contact. Even if the contract is unfavorable, you are not likely to be in a position to make major changes, at least not in the short term.

Manufacturing processes Again you are not likely to be able to examine issues in great detail in preliminary due diligence, but a survey of the facilities, equipment, and grounds can give you a lot of cues about how up-to-date the equipment is (and thus how costly to replace or modernize, if necessary). The facilities can also give you some clues as to employee attitudes and morale—whether things are kept neat, people are at work or standing around, and the demeanor of employees as you pass through the plant.

Environmental issues Environmental impact is another area of growing importance. Some larger companies may have an environmental study recently done and on file. But with many smaller and older companies, the owner may not even be aware of problems that exist. You may or may not discover some of these problems until the formal due diligence phase. In the case of one company explored by JPE Inc., a pollution problem stemmed from underground tanks removed years earlier. A concrete slab factory floor had been built over the original site, making it even more costly to investigate. Studies carried out during formal due diligence eventually revealed that the problem was a relatively minor one, but the investigation itself was time-consuming and costly.

You should seriously consider dropping a company with major environmental pollution problems unless it is possible to assess the cost and extent of cleanup accurately before closing. Even if the former owner is legally liable, it is often very difficult to collect from any but the largest corporations after closing takes place. If you are able to assess the probably cost, you can factor the cost into the price or into an escrow agreement that holds the money for potential cleanup in a separate account for a designated period after the closing.

Tax implications Another very important area to investigate during preliminary due diligence are the tax implications of the sale for the seller. Tax laws change over time. You need to investigate early on, with the help of a qualified tax lawyer, what the tax implications are from the standpoint of *both* buyer and seller. Sometimes, once a seller looks at his taxes, he is not so sure he wants to sell his company after all. For instance, he may net much less money than he counted on for retirement and decide to continue working instead.

Red Flags / Surprises to Watch for During Due Diligence

Several red flags are most common to come across during preliminary or formal due diligence. If the answer to any of the following questions is yes, you might want to seriously consider discontinuing your investigation and look for another company with fewer problems:

1. Does the company have serious environmental problems, ground, water, or air pollution that might be costly to rectify?
2. Is there significant labor unrest and/or a labor contract about to be renegotiated?
3. Does the owner have too high expectations about the price?
4. Is there too much debt?
5. Are there potentially serious product liability issues?
6. Are there employee grievances that may lead to a costly lawsuit?

There will be some surprises. Stay calm and collected. It is not unusual. Look at them, study them, get a clear understanding of what they are and what they mean to the business. Evaluate them. Do not let the seller feel that you will walk away from the deal every time you have a surprise. After all, the negotiating/acquisition process is a series of problem-solving undertaking. To minimize surprises, be as prepared as you can and be within the timetable you have. Send the seller a detailed list of what you and your team want to review. Do not start the process until you have what you need.

Chapter Summary

This chapter reviews the important step of preliminary due diligence that takes place once a confidentiality agreement is signed, and you are satisfied that a lead meets your major criteria. The preliminary due diligence has three important aspects: a meeting with the seller, one or two company visits, and a preliminary review of documentation.

There are four key goals in the preliminary due diligence phase. They are the following:

1. To determine whether this company is what you want to buy (barring any unexpected "skeletons" you might uncover during formal due diligence)
2. To determine the price you want to offer in your letter of intent
3. To determine whether the seller is serious about selling and why
4. To develop rapport with the seller

There is a variety of information, which you can gather at this stage without spending a lot of money by reviewing available documentation and visiting the company. During preliminary due diligence, you want to get an overall sense of the company's financial condition, marketing and sales, employee practices, manufacturing processes, and very important but sometimes overlooked, environmental issues. Basically, you inherit any potential liabilities that are buried in the information that the seller provides. And if the seller lacks deep pockets, you can still be sued for problems that you inherited but did not cause. The earlier you surface those skeletons, if they are there, the less time you waste on a company that is perhaps best to pass over.

You also carry out preliminary due diligence to get a more accurate estimate of the price you plan to offer to make sure that you and the seller are not too far apart.

The next chapter picks up where this chapter leaves off with the drafting of a letter of intent and formal due diligence.

CHAPTER 10

LETTER OF INTENT AND
FORMAL DUE DILIGENCE

This chapter covers the letter of intent, which should be negotiated and signed prior to the start of formal due diligence and the formal due diligence process itself.

The most extensive and expensive investigation of a company lead takes place during the *formal due diligence*. Formal due diligence can be viewed as the fourth filter through which company leads pass. Because of its expense, you should probably plan to complete formal due diligence on a company you are fairly certain to buy. Sometimes the process of negotiating the letter of intent itself weeds out some candidates that look good after preliminary due diligence. Or you may uncover information during the formal due diligence that you were not aware of during the preliminary due diligence phase. It is likely that during the eighteenth-month to two-year period you are scrutinizing company leads, that out of two dozen leads subjected to a thorough preliminary due diligence, only four or five will actually follow through to formal due diligence. Some will drop out during the preliminary due diligence phase itself. Other company leads might drop out because buyer and seller are unable to agree on terms in the letter of intent.

Letter of Intent

The *letter of intent* is a nonbinding expression of intent, with the exception of certain provisions that are binding, similar in this way to the letter of interest. However, it is usually much more detailed than the letter of interest. Generally, a company will not allow the prospective buyer to speak with customers, employees, or suppliers or to conduct environmental studies until the letter of intent is signed. Since many of the details that are described in the letter of intent are addressed in the final purchase agreement, the letter of intent also serves the purpose of moving the buyer and seller toward a meeting of the minds.

Purpose of the Letter of Intent

There are two key purposes of the letter of intent. First, it is to get a commitment from the seller that he will not negotiate with anybody else or solicit offers during a specified period of time while the buyer is carrying out formal due diligence. This is very important since you are likely to spend a significant amount of money and effort during the formal due diligence period and need protection from the possibility that the seller would sell to someone else.

Secondly, although the letter of intent does not bind either the seller or the buyer to consummate the transaction, its purpose is also to create an atmosphere of good faith between buyer and seller to move forward toward a completed agreement. Sometimes, this "good faith" is reinforced by an agreement to pay a break-up fee, a penalty paid by either side if it decides not to go through with the sale, regardless of the reason.

Timing of the Letter of Intent

The letter of intent is typically negotiated after you have completed preliminary due diligence but before you embark on formal due diligence. When an investment banker is involved, the letter of intent is usually stated as a specific requirement to be signed within a relatively short period after the letter of interest is accepted. Whether or not the seller insists upon it, you should generally negotiate and sign a letter of intent before carrying out formal due diligence to protect against the possibility that the seller might solicit and/or negotiate deals with other prospective buyers.

Main Sections of the Letter of Intent

The letter of intent has four main sections: the purchase price, break-up fee, contingencies, and exclusivity clause. Exhibit 10.1 provides a sample letter of intent.

Price and what is included in sale The letter of intent, although nonbinding on price, should ideally reflect the agreed-upon price as accurately as possible. Otherwise, you run a greater risk of the deal going sour at the last minute.

In agreeing upon the price, the letter of intent also spells out exactly what you are buying for that price. For instance in the example in exhibit 10.1, you should list the assets to be acquired as well as the liabilities to be assumed from the seller.

In paragraph 4 of the sample letter, the letter of intent also spells out the percentage of the total price to be paid at closing and the percentage to be withheld until after closing pending an audit of the balance sheet as of the date of closing reflecting the exact value of the company at closing. The actual amount of funds transferred at closing is further reduced by an amount to be negotiated between buyer and seller that is set in an escrow account for a negotiated period after closing to cover any damages resulting from a breach of the seller's representations and warranties contained in the purchase agreement.

Closing The letter of intent should clarify when closing will take place. In the sample letter in exhibit 10.1, closing is tied to satisfactory completion of formal due diligence by the buyer and government approval of the sale, if required by the Hart-Scott-Rodino Act. Usually the latter is required when the company size of either the seller or buyer is above $100 million in either revenues or assets. If required, you are advised to file under the Hart-Scott-Rodino Act at the letter of intent stage. This reduces the delay that might be caused while you wait for government approval.

Access to information The letter of intent also spells out the obligations the seller has to provide access to various documents and individuals. For instance, in the sample agreement, the seller is obligated to provide access to the books, records, facilities, personnel, customers, and suppliers relating to the business of the seller. Documents must include collective bargaining agreements and any related collective bargaining materials.

Break-up fee The letter of intent may sometimes specify a break-up fee, an amount of money to be paid if the sale does not go through. The break-up fee, if included, can apply to the seller only, the buyer only, or to both buyer and seller, depending upon the wording of the contract. When there is no break-up fee, as in the sample letter of intent in exhibit 10.1, you are not liable as a buyer for any damages for breaking off the negotiations unless the seller can prove you did not act in good faith.

A break-up fee is probably not needed in the case of the investment-banker—brokered deal. In that case, the seller is clearly motivated to sell and has incurred his or her own expenses in the selling process. When dealing with a private individual that is not going through an investment banker, especially with a more informal intermediary, it becomes increasingly critical to negotiate this type of clause. You don't want to be in the position of spending $50,000 or more on due diligence only to have a seller change his or her mind about selling the company.

Exclusivity rights An exclusivity rights clause is usually included in the letter of intent. This prevents the seller from soliciting other buyers or negotiating in any other way with other buyers. In the example presented in exhibit 10.1, the buyer has exclusive rights for ninety days.

Nondisclosure In the case of a publicly traded company, the United States securities laws restrict anyone with any nonpublic information about the possible sale of the company from either buying or selling stock of the public company or communicating that information to anyone else who is likely to buy or sell such securities. This paragraph is included to inform the seller that any information related to the possible purchase must therefore be kept confidential and that anyone aware of the transaction be prevented from buying or selling stock.

Altering the Letter of Intent Prior to Closing

Sometimes, as a result of due diligence, you may uncover information that leads you to change your valuation of the company and what price you are willing to pay. Although the letter of intent itself is usually not amended, you are advised to develop a paper trail of correspondence. Since the letter of intent is nonbinding, you do not need to formally amend the document as you would a purchase agreement or other document, but written documentation reduces the risk of a misunderstanding later that might prevent the closing from taking place.

Formal Due Diligence

Due diligence is the most critical phase of the acquisition process for *buying the right company*. Your decision to proceed further with negotiations, how much to pay for it, and close the deal will depend to a great extent on the detailed understanding of the candidate business that will come from a thorough due diligence. Given how critical this phase of the process is, the buyer must be prepared not to rush, to be prepared for surprises, and to cope with such surprises by staying calm and determining their significance to the business. The buyer should further realize that the vast majority of prospective buyers who fail to close a deal probably do so either because they get cold feet when they unexpected facts surface, or run back and forth to the seller so much that the seller backs off from the deal. As you will see in this chapter, due diligence is not only a review of financial and accounting information though these are extremely important, it also involves all the facets of the business, people, suppliers, customers, company / product / services image, technology, management and production processes.

You do not want to embark upon formal due diligence until a letter of intent is negotiated and signed by both parties. At the same time, you must be prepared to begin due diligence immediately upon signing, especially if the exclusivity rights clause that you have negotiated is set for a finite period.

The Legal Implications of Due Diligence

Legally, while the seller is responsible for providing you with information, it is your responsibility to review and evaluate this information for accuracy and completeness. If the seller provides you with information without withholding damaging facts, you will have a very difficult time suing the seller later for damages, even if this information is buried within hundreds or even thousands of pages of documentation. The law basically only requires the seller to provide the buyer with the information, *not* to point it out to you. If it is buried within legalese or accounting terminology you do not understand, you will still have no recourse in the courts. And even if you do have grounds to sue, i.e., you can prove a problem had been hidden from you, you may have a difficult time collecting from the previous owner unless the seller was a very large company.

In short, although a very thorough evaluation of even a midsized company can become very costly, it is still less expensive than finding yourself saddled with an underperforming company, or worse, perhaps a lawsuit costing you several hundreds of thousands or even millions of dollars.

Content and Steps in Formal Due Diligence

This section reviews some of the key components of the formal due diligence.

A complete and thorough due diligence can cost anywhere between $50,000 and over $100,000. Obviously, for a very small business, you may be able to carry out the investigation more economically. Regardless of company size, certain basic issues should be investigated.

Exhibit 10.2 is an example that lists in more detail the different activities that should be conducted in a formal due diligence, with an estimated budget for conducting the due diligence for a medium-sized company. The main categories in which the information is grouped are the following: the reason the company is for sale; key strategic factors; products/services and marketing; production, purchasing, operations and facilities; labor and other personnel; financial and accounting considerations; management background, experience, style and practices; and legal matters.

Although a cursory review of many of the issues listed in exhibit 10.2 may take place during the preliminary due diligence, the coverage during formal due diligence should be thorough and complete. In our experience, it is not unusual for this phase of effort to cost well over $100,000 depending on the size and complexity of the business. However, these are generally for companies with over $50 million in revenues. The due diligence costs will be somewhat proportionately lower for a smaller company prospect. However, certain fixed costs are involved with the various consultants you may need to do a thorough and accurate job.

Here we list fifteen typical steps for a formal due diligence process. The activities are listed in chronological order although their weight in the overall decision may be different (see priority rating in column three in exhibit 10.2).

Step 1: Evaluate management To start with, the acquisition team interviews and evaluates *key* members of management to understand their roles in the prospective company and their effectiveness. Depending upon the size of company, you are not likely to want to replace all your key people in the organization. You will benefit from purchasing a company where you can retain a competent management team.

Step 2: Review product lines and marketing The second step is to review and analyze the product lines and other marketing information. Sales backlog, trends in historical financial performance including sales and profitability, industry conditions and competition are very important factors that you want to explore early on.

Step 3: Review operations You will also want to review the company's operations. The goal is to identify potential cost savings and to corroborate the amount of cost savings you have already estimated.

Step 4: Review compensation and benefits Step 4 involves a review of the company's compensation structure and benefits programs.

Step 5: Financial audit The next step is to review the financial audit and any accounting or tax issues.

Step 6: Scrutinize unusual tax returns Step 6 involves closer scrutiny of any unusual aspects of the tax returns.

Step 7: Evaluate risk management In step 7, you review the risk management issues. This includes, but is not limited to product warranty, health care, and workers' compensation.

Step 8: Review intercompany transactions Step 8 is a review of the company's intercompany transactions.

Step 9: Review inventory and production control systems Step 9 is a review of the company's inventory and production control systems and all other significant management information systems.

Step 10: Prepare a break-even analysis In step 10, you prepare and review a break-even analysis based on your expected cost and capital structure, which may be quite different than the seller's current structure.

Step 11: Interview customers and suppliers Step 11 is to interview customers and suppliers. Although often a rich source of information, you may be denied early access to customers and suppliers, at least until a letter of intent is signed and accepted.

Step 12: Review research and engineering Step 12 involves a review of the nature and extent of research and engineering expenditures to determine their effectiveness.

Step 13: Identify issues for purchase agreement Step 13 is to compile a list of issues to be considered when drafting the purchase agreement. These might include various representations and warranties and related escrow agreements for potential liabilities and other problems that you may not foresee being resolved by the day of closing.

Step 14: Review valuation of accounts receivables and inventories Step 14 constitutes a review of accounts receivable and inventories for potential valuation problems.

Step 15: Review corporate controls Step 15 is a review of internal and operational controls and a general assessment of their reliability.

Other items to obtain during due diligence Exhibit 10.2 also lists the items that you should retain legal counsel to cover. Exhibit 10.3 includes a sample document request list for due diligence, based on the list used by JPI Inc. and JPE Inc.

Consultants Recommended for Due Diligence

To carry out due diligence accurately, you are likely to need outside consultants to help you unless you have this expertise within your management team. Some key consultants needed are discussed in this section.

Financial Auditor Even if you are a private company buying another private company, it is very useful to have an auditor come in to check the accuracy of the books. A good auditor might uncover such problems as inflated inventory or understated salaries . . .

Environmental consultant Current environmental laws in the US and several other countries make it imperative that you investigate the company you plan to purchase to be sure it does not have any hidden environmental problems even if no real property is involved in the sale. Whether the property is owned or leased, the company would be responsible as an "owner/operator." In addition, the company is responsible for its hazardous wastes disposed of off-site.

Not all environmental damage is easy to detect. Problems might be covered over with new buildings. The problems may be buried deep within the earth. You want to work with a consultant who specializes in requirements of the environmental protection agencies.

Risk specialist You also need to involve someone who can review all the risk insurances including product liability, fire insurance, property insurance, or any other transferable insurance.

Employee benefits You may need separate consultants to evaluate group medical insurance plans and the transferability of available plans to a new owner, as well as pension and other welfare benefits plans.

Legal You will continue to need legal expertise during the formal due diligence phase, not only to review documents, but also to begin negotiation of the purchase agreement, which should take place concurrently.

Other Activities Taking Place During Due Diligence

While due diligence is taking place, it is strongly advisable to carry out three other activities concurrently: development of the final purchase agreement; finalizing your bank loan, if needed; and development of the operational plan for implementation on the day of closing.

The Development of the Final Purchase Agreement

As soon as the letter of intent is signed and due diligence begins, you will usually find it very valuable to begin work on the final purchase agreement. The exception to this might be if you are really bothered by something that might affect your decision to buy the company, then you might complete that part of due diligence first before you spend legal fees to begin drafting the purchase agreement. But barring such a problem, you should move in parallel, both to save time and to obtain information useful to you during the due diligence process itself.

Unlike the letter of interest and letter of intent, the acquisition purchase agreement is a legally binding agreement. There are serious consequences of misrepresenting the business in the purchase agreement. For this reason, the negotiation process that takes place while drafting the purchase agreement can contribute to your accurate understanding of the business. In particular, the representations and warranties section of the purchase agreement is a critical part of the due diligence process itself.

For instance, the purchase agreement spells out that there are no liabilities other than those disclosed. The warranty says that if there are additional liabilities that have not been disclosed, the seller is responsible for reimbursing the buyer, even after the sale, if he or she knew about these liabilities beforehand. In negotiating this clause, sometimes you find a seller that becomes uncomfortable at this point and does not want to sign such a statement. You may enter into a dialogue that begins to turn up issues that the seller had been afraid to raise earlier. In this way, you often hear more about the company in the process. For instance, the information might relate to disgruntled employees who have threatened (but perhaps not yet filed) a lawsuit. If indeed that employee later sues, the seller might be held liable for the lawsuit if he or she failed to disclose the problem at this stage.

In sum, the seller frequently waits until he or she is almost ready to sign the purchase agreement before revealing all the known problems about the company. Up to that point, there is no liability for them as long they are negotiating in good faith and have not disclosed any nonpublic information to outsiders or solicited deals with other buyers. It is not until you actually begin negotiating the purchase agreement that you can start putting teeth or muscle into the seller's representations about his or her company. By doing so, you can learn a lot about the company.

Late disclosure is not always a matter of dishonesty. The questions, which surface in formal due diligence may be new to the owner or at least issues he or she has not stayed on top of or thought about recently. For instance, in the US, you should ask whether or not there are any problems conforming with the Occupational Safety and Health Act (OSHA). The owner may have forgotten that an OSHA inspector was out six months ago and perhaps never talked to the foreman to find out whether a particular problem was fixed.

In sum, negotiating the representations and warranties section of the purchase agreement, which can be several pages in length, often brings out a lot of information useful to the due diligence process. The due diligence benefit of the representations and warranties section may actually outweigh the liability benefit. If you do learn about the problem later, although the owner is liable for damages, you are probably facing a time-consuming and expensive legal process to collect. You have to prove that the owner knew and intentionally misled you about a problem. It is much easier to find out about such problems prior to closing and has the added benefit of allowing you to use such issues in renegotiating the purchase price.

Finalizing the Financing

In addition to working on the final purchase agreement, you will also find it useful to work with your lenders during this period. Even if you have a line of credit, there are certain requirements that a lender might expect for this particular deal. If the company you are purchasing is your first one, the issues will be different than if you are adding the acquisition to an existing company. In the latter case, the lender will be interested in the impact that the acquisition will have on your existing company's balance sheet. Chapter 13: Financing the Acquisition will explore some of these issues in greater detail.

Developing the Action Plan

The due diligence process, if done correctly, will reveal a variety of areas requiring attention, both in the short-term and in the long run. Thus, the due diligence process provides you with the opportunity to begin development of the operational action plan you plan to implement at closing.

Employees are a valuable source for pointing out areas in need of attention whether they be improvements in operations or changes in the marketing plan. It is advisable to involve management level people closely, especially those who plan to stay on with the company after the ownership changes hands. Chapter 15 will explore this topic in greater detail.

Chapter Summary

This chapter covers the letter of intent, which should be negotiated and signed prior to the start of the formal due diligence process itself.

The *letter of intent* is similar to the letter of interest, although the buyer is cautioned that typically he or she must also agree to certain binding provisions in case he or she backs out of the deal later. But it is a necessary step since generally, a company will not allow the prospective buyer to speak with customers, employees, or suppliers or to conduct environmental studies until the letter of intent is signed. Since many of the details that are described in the letter of intent are addressed in the final purchase agreement, the letter of intent also serves the purpose of moving the buyer and seller toward a meeting of the minds.

Due diligence is the most critical phase of the acquisition process for *buying the right company*. Your decision to proceed further with negotiations, how much to pay for it and close the deal will depend to a great extent on the detailed understanding of the candidate business that will come from a thorough due diligence. Especially during the formal due diligence phase, the buyer must be prepared for unexpected information. A great many deals go sour either because the buyer overreacts to certain surprises or otherwise behaves so erratically from the seller's point of view that the seller decides to back away from the deal. Staying cool and calm during this phase is critical if the buyer wants to avoid wasting the time and expense invested to this point in identifying a candidate for purachase.

Exhibit 10.1. A sample letter of intent

[Date]

Confidential

We appreciate the opportunities we have been given to meet with management and visit the facilities of _____ ("Seller"). Based upon those meetings and the information you have provided us, _____ ("Buyer") is pleased to submit a proposal to buy all of the assets of Seller, shown on the attached balance sheet dated _____ ("Balance Sheet"), a copy of which is marked exhibit A and attached hereto. The following are the basic terms of Buyer's proposal.

1. Assets to be Acquired. [All] assets owned by Seller, including, but not limited to, the assets listed on the attached Balance Sheet as of [date of closing], 20x6; _____ _____ ("Assets").

2. *Liabilities to be Assumed.* _____ _____ ("Assumed Liabilities"). Other than as specifically agreed, Buyer shall not assume, and shall be indemnified by Seller for, any liability, whether or not accrued and whether known or unknown, arising from the operation of the Business prior to the Closing.

3. Purchase Price. The purchase price will be $_____ adjusted for changes in the Balance Sheet from _____ from the date of the agreement to the date of closing; plus the assumption of the liabilities described in Paragraph 2 hereof.

4. Payment of the Purchase Price. At the closing, Buyer will pay cash equal to ____% of the Purchase Price (____% being withheld pending the purchase price adjustment provided in Paragraph 5, below), minus an amount to be negotiated between Buyer and Seller, which will be placed into an escrow account for a period to be negotiated to protect Buyer in the event of damages resulting from a breach of Seller's representations and warranties contained in the Asset Purchase Agreement.

5. *Purchase Price Adjustment.* As a public reporting company, Buyer will required audited financial statements of Seller to include in Buyer's

filings with the Securities and Exchange Commission. Therefore, in order to fulfill such requirements, and to serve as the vehicle for the purchase price adjustment, promptly following the closing, Buyer will cause an audited balance sheet of the business as of the date of closing ("Closing Balance Sheet") to be prepared at Buyer's sole expense by Buyer's independent certified public accountants. Seller may, at its sole expense, have its independent certified public accountants observe the taking of the physical inventory and audit the balance sheet. The Closing Balance Sheet shall be prepared in accordance with generally accepted accounting principles and shall fairly present the financial position of Seller as of the close of business on the day preceding the date of closing. Seller shall have 30 days following its receipt of the Closing Balance Sheet in which to object, in writing and in reasonable detail, thereto. If within 30 days of Buyer's receipt of Seller's objections Buyer and Seller are unable to agree to a resolution of the differences, the Closing Balance Sheet will be submitted to a neutral arbitrator, mutually agreed upon and who shall be partner of a widely recognized accounting firm, for final and binding arbitration.

6. *Closing.* The closing may e held within the later of (i) days after Buyer's satisfactory completion of due diligence, and (ii) 10 days following receipt of government approval under Hart-Scott-Rodino or the expiration of the 30-day waiting period there under without comment.

7. *Other Conditions.*

    a. Seller shall have provided Buyer and its principal lender, together with their respective attorneys, accountants and agents, with access to the books, records, facilities, personnel, customers and suppliers relating to the business of Seller, and Buyer shall have reasonably satisfied itself and such lender with respect thereto.

    b. Seller shall have provided Buyer and its attorneys, accountants, and agents with access to Seller's collective bargaining agreements, records pertaining thereto, and the Union's representatives, and Buyer shall have reviewed to the contents of the collective bargaining agreement and records, the obligations created by such agreements, the condition of Seller's labor relations, and the continuity of Seller's employee base to determine their acceptability to Buyer.

c. Buyer shall have obtained additional debt [equity] financing in an amount and on terms reasonably satisfactory to Buyer.

8. *Exclusivity Rights.* Seller agrees that unless sooner terminated by the parties, for a period of 90 days, it will not, directly or indirectly, through any officer, director, shareholder, employee, agent or otherwise, (i) solicit or initiate, directly or indirectly, or encourage submission of inquiries, proposals or offers from any potential buyer (other than Buyer) relating to the disposition of the capital stock, assets or business, or any part thereof (other than sales of inventory in the ordinary course of business), or (ii) participate in any discussions or negotiations regarding, or furnish to any person, the information with respect to the disposition of the capital stock or assets of Seller's business.

9. *Non-Disclosure.* Without the prior written consent of Buyer, Seller will not disclose to any person who does not have a "need-to-know" either the contents of this letter or the fact that discussions regarding the transactions contemplated by this letter are taking place. Seller, including its officers, directors, shareholders and representatives, are hereby advised that Buyer is a publicly traded company and that the United States securities laws restrict persons with material nonpublic information about a company obtained directly or indirectly from that company from purchasing or selling securities of such company, or from communicating such information to any other person under circumstances in which it is reasonably foreseeable that such person is likely to purchase or sell such securities.

10. *Non-Binding Contract.* This letter is intended to reflect the general terms of the offer contained herein and upon acceptance shall be deemed a letter of intent pursuant to which Buyer and Seller will negotiate a definitive Asset Purchase Agreement. This letter shall not be deemed or construed to constitute a purchase agreement and shall create no binding obligations other than the obligations of Seller pursuant to Paragraphs 8 and 9 above.

11. *Acceptance.* If the foregoing general terms are acceptable to Seller, please so indicate by signing the enclosed copy of this letter and returning it to the undersigned. Upon acceptance, Buyer will promptly begin its due diligence, instruct its attorneys to prepare the necessary

contract documents, and seek board of directors approval for the transaction. If the offer reflected in this letter is not accepted prior to 4:00 p.m. local time, [estimated closing date], the offer shall be deemed withdrawn without any further action by Seller.

Very truly yours,

BUYER

By: _____
   Its:

Accepted and agreed to this _____ day of _____.

SELLER

By: _____
   Its:

Exhibit 10.2.

A SAMPLE DUE DILIGENCE PROGRAM

	CHRONOLOGICAL	PRIORITY	ESTIMATED COST
1.	Interview and evaluate key members of management to understand their roles in the Company and their effectiveness.	1	$5,000-7,000
2.	Review and analyze product lines (i.e., gross profit analysis), sales backlog, trends in historical financial performance, markets, industry conditions and competition to independently support the reasonableness of buyer's forecast.	2	$13,500-26,500
3.	Evaluate the Company's operation in the area of plant and facilities, production, purchasing and inventories. The goal is to identify potential cost savings and to corroborate the amount of cost savings estimated	3	$5,000-9,500
4.	Review the Company's compensation structure and benefit programs for both salaried and hourly workers to determine whether employee costs will remain reasonably stable and to determine if there are any unrecorded liabilities (e.g., post-employment medical benefits are currently not required to be recorded under generally accepted accounting principles).	9	$7,500-9.500
5.	Review audit and tax work-papers for the last two years, including quarterly review work-papers, to identify potential accounting, tax and internal control issues.	10	$3,000-6,000

6.	Review state and federal tax returns for unusual elections, review IRS audit reports, determine extent of tax exposure issues, identify state and local tax exposure related to non-filing and underreporting.	7	$7,500-8,500
7.	Review risk management issues including, but not limited to, product warranty, health care and workers' compensation.	5	$5,000-6,500
8.	Review the nature of the Company's inter-company transactions and transfer pricing.	14	$5,000-6,500
9.	Review the Company's inventory and production control systems and all other significant management information systems.	13	$7,500-9,500
10.	Prepare and review a break-even analysis based on Buyer's expected cost and capital structure.	11	$7,500-10,000
11.	Interview customers and suppliers.	4	$5,000-7,000
12.	Review the nature and extent of research and engineering expenditures to determine the effectiveness of Company programs.	15	$2,500-3,500
13.	Compile a list of issues to be considered when drafting the purchase agreement.	12	$2,500-5,000
14.	Review accounts receivable and inventories a) for potential valuation problems and b) collateral limitations. Review payable and accruals for age and understanding of content.	6	$4,500-6,000
15.	Review internal and operational control environment and make a general assessment of reliability.	8	$1,000-2,000
	TOTAL		$82,000-$123,000

	Retain legal counsel to cover these items - Review the corporate structure (articles of incorporation, bylaws, minutes books) and identify states in which they are qualified to do business; - Review all financial agreements; - Union matters - Leases - Intellectual property - Tangible assets (e.g. status and title of all real estate and perform a UCC search); - Legal proceedings; - Regulatory issues (e.g., environmental and OSHA); - Hart-Scott-Roding filing; - Prepare purchase agreement.		

Exhibit 10.3. A sample document request list for due diligence

SALES / MARKETING

Five-year record of product sales performance

Three- to five-year forecast of sales for the company and estimated share of market

Summary of special discounts and credit terms offered to significant customers.

Number of customers and terms of sales

List of top twenty customers with five years' sales history (or sufficient number to include 50% of sales)

Special customer price programs, formal or informal

Customer rebate programs, formal or informal

Copies of sales collateral material, price books, company brochures, etc.

MANUFACTURING

Appraisals of the company's properties and fixed assets

Location of plant or plants

Description and layout of plant and property

Land information including a. Acreage b. Cost c. Assessed value d. Fair market value appraisal

Detailed schedule of manufacturing overhead for most recent three years

List of major materials and supplies purchased and annual amounts purchased

List of patents and trademarks owned, licenses granted and amount and history or royalties received

ACCOUNTING / FINANCIAL

Audited financial statements for last five years including the independent accountant management letters on internal controls and contingent liabilities

If more than one subsidiary or division, comparative financial results for each profit and loss or cost unit for the five years

Unaudited financial statements for most recent reporting period year to date

Most recent budget and/or projected operating and financial statements.

Trends in inventory levels by reporting category for at least past three years (i.e., raw materials, work in process, finished goods, etc.)

Stratification into fast-moving, slow-moving, excess, and obsolete inventory

Inventory turnover (ratio of average inventory to cost of sales) for at least past three years

Percentage relation of material costs to sales—last five years

Relationship of raw material to goods bought for resale

Accounting manual, instructions, and chart of accounts

Unfunded service costs of pension plans

HUMAN RESOURCES

Number of persons employed and major areas of activity

Chart of organization and related salaries, employment contracts, if any

Policy manual, if any

Number of employees by sex and age groupings showing separately those in production, sales, purchasing, engineering, administration, etc.

Approximate total wage and salary cost of each category

All union affiliations and contracts, including:

> Name of union(s)
> Employees covered
> Length of contract
> Expiration date

Average pay scale and fringe benefits for production employees for at least three years

Any formal charges pending before federal or state labor agencies

Details of employment agreements or unwritten understandings

Pension plans, profit-sharing plans, life insurance, disability insurance, medical benefits, travel and accident plans. Funding status of plans, if appropriate

Stock option or stock bonus plans and outstanding options

LEGAL / CORPORATE

Articles of incorporation and bylaws of the company

List of officers

List of directors, affiliations, ages and years as director

Capitalization; stock distribution—number of shareholders and names of principle shareholders; rights of each class of stock; stockholders' agreements, etc.

List of subsidiaries and details of business conducted

Name, addresses, and contacts of company's professional advisors:

> Attorneys
> Auditors
> Principle banking relationship
> Investment bankers

Contingent liabilities:

Warranty policy and current status of outstanding cases

Product liability

Environmental matters (EPA, state, etc.)—compliance, legal exposure, possible violations, cleanup obligations, fines and penalties, etc

Union contracts

Any other pending or threatened litigation

CHAPTER 11

VALUING AND PRICING THE COMPANY

Before you can begin final negotiations on price, you need to determine the value of the company. You can use several techniques to value a company. We recommend the discounted cash flow value approach as the most accurate method although other approaches are useful in preliminary stages of your search to give you a sense of the range of the estimated price.

Timing and Scope of the Valuation Process

An initial calculation of valuation can be done on a fairly mechanical basis, based on information provided to you by the seller using established formulae and guidelines. However, determining the accuracy of the financial data that the seller provides you is an ongoing part of the evaluation process that should take place throughout preliminary and formal due diligence up to the closing. Thus, valuation takes place along with negotiations throughout the deal-making process. One of the key objectives of due diligence is to surface any information that might affect the accurate valuation of the company. If your team does not have a financial auditor, you should hire one to verify the accuracy of the historical data.

Once you verify the completeness and accuracy of existing documents, historical valuation of a company is often relatively easy from a technical standpoint. But it may be a fairly inaccurate reflection of what you can expect from the firm's financial performance in the future. Thus, although a preliminary valuation of the company might be done initially when you first receive financial data from the company, refining the financial assumptions about the company's future performance must take into consideration a wide array of nonfinancial considerations. Accurate forecasting requires a thorough understanding of general trends as well, trends specific to your industry, the economy, and of course, a thorough understanding of the strengths and weaknesses of the particular company you plan to purchase.

General trends First of all, you should consider any social, technological, economic, political, or legal trends that might affect future growth or decline of your company or industry.

Societal and lifestyle changes can also impact a company. A growing population of senior citizens opens the door to more rapidly expanding health-care related fields.

New competition or opportunities may come from outside your industry as new technologies emerge. For instance, the television industry by the end of the first decade of the 21st century witnessed increased competition from the alternatives provided by much more flexible and diverse internet downloadable programming.

You also need to watch for changing economic patterns. In exploring economic trends, consider the business cycle for your particular industry as well as more general swings in the local, regional or national economies in which you may do business.

No business today can afford to ignore ever changing political and legal trends. They may create new problems, but they can also spell new opportunity. For instance, a ruling that cab drivers do not need to have a state license in Colorado has spurred a number of new cab businesses in that state while putting some long established companies in some amount of jeopardy, reducing their monopolistic position.

The concern about the environment and environmental pollution has grown to the point that you may need to consider not only what the political and legal requirements are, but the expectations of the surrounding community, standards of which at times may exceed the minimum that the law requires. Appropriate disposal of current waste, environmental toxins that workers might be exposed to and hidden problems from wastes improperly disposed of in the past all need to be closely scrutinized.

Understanding industry trends and the immediate competition
Beyond the general trends, there are likely to be trends in your own industry, globally, nationally, regionally, and locally. To avoid being blindsided, you need to consider competition from each of these angles. Businesses are often sold because a historically profitable firm is being threatened by new competition that the former owner is not sure how to respond. It does not mean that you should not buy a particular business, but you had better be prepared to respond to tougher competition.

Understanding of the company itself In valuing the company, you also need to consider the myriad issues already presented in the formal due diligence chapter. For instance, thorough due diligence may uncover somewhat artificially inflated short-term profit data because equipment and facility renewal may have been deferred by the current owner.

In reviewing the company you plan to purchase, you need to consider its potential strengths and weaknesses in all the areas covered by due diligence. In addition, you may want to consider the areas in which it is very capable and the areas in which it is weak. In today's marketplace, being average is often no longer enough to maintain one's competitive position. A company must excel in areas important to the customers it serves, whether it is maintaining a discount price, fast service, high quality, or all three. Many companies espouse these goals, but meeting these goals requires that the company builds in its capabilities in its marketing, production, management or in other aspects of operations. The future value of the company depends on the quality of functioning of the organization as an overall system, not on the particular assets it may have sitting in the warehouse or the orders in the sales department's desk at a particular moment in time.

Pricing versus Valuing

Valuation and pricing are not the same. The company's *value* is what it will be worth with the improvements that the buyer plans to make to improve the company's performance. The company's *price* is the amount that the buyer is willing to pay the seller for the company, regardless of its worth.

Why are price and value not exactly the same? There are several factors that might influence the price.

How motivated is the seller? An eager seller, perhaps someone with health problems impatient to settle his or her estate, may be willing to sell for a price below the company's market value. An unmotivated seller, one that perhaps had no intentions of selling until approached by a convincing broker to show his company to the buyer, may require a price higher than market value before he or she is willing to sell.

How will the company be financed? If the buyer is depending heavily on borrowed funds from a bank, he or she is not likely to get approval on a loan for a company that is priced much above market value. If the buyer needs to pay off the debt from the company's cash flow, this will be closely scrutinized as well. On the other hand, if the deal is largely a cash transaction between private parties, a bank's opinion of the company's value will not interfere with closing. Of course, a buyer should proceed cautiously whenever paying well above market value but is less tied to the bank's opinion when no banker is involved.

What is likely to happen to business in the near future? Although the discounted cash flow technique is more apt to reflect future earnings than some of the other methods in any industry, the future is difficult to predict with total accuracy. An industry predicted to head into a downturn is likely to command a softer price than an industry that is fairly clearly headed for strong, steady growth in the next three to five years.

What are the tax implications for both buyer and seller? Finally, another factor to consider in the price are the tax implications of the sale for both the buyer and seller. If the transaction is structured in a certain way to improve the taxable position of the seller, this can affect the value. Also, if there are tax benefits available to the buyer, he or she may be willing to pay a higher price.

Different Methods for Determining a Company's Price

Calculating the value of a business can be complicated. However, there are business appraisers available to assist in this process. For example, in the US, certified members of the American Society of Appraisers and/or the Institute of Business Appraisers Inc. can be of help.

Different authors will argue the benefits and disadvantages of the basic techniques for pricing a business. For midsized companies, Lawrence Tuller identifies four common ways to value a going business:[8]

1. Profitability or multiple net earnings method—which is based on a multiple of net profits
2. Net asset value—a very conservative method that looks only at the assets of the company, without counting value for goodwill
3. Historical cash flow—valuation based on the cash flow generated in the past; and
4. Discounted cash flow method—the forecast of the cash obtained in the future

In addition, the banks might look at the *liquidation* value of a company, the value of all assets if sold off immediately, especially for a loan they might consider as a high-risk value. This approach is even more conservative than the net asset approach because inventory and other assets are discounted heavily, assuming that a quick liquidation would require sale of assets at well below market value.

Within each of these general approaches, variations in computational technique may further lead to different results. Which is the best approach?

---

[8]   L.W. Tuller, *Buying In: A Complete Guide to Acquiring a Business or Professional Practice*. Liberty Hall, 1990.

If your criterion is ease of calculation, the multiple net earnings method might well be the simplest. The discounted cash flow method is viewed by some experts as too complicated to use, but by others as the only accurate technique for valuing companies. Let's explore these different techniques in turn.

The Profitability Ratio

One takes the after-tax profit from the previous year, uses a price/earnings ratio from a similar but publicly traded company and arrives at a value. For example,

After-tax profit last year	$ 2,000
Assuming a P/E ratio of	x 5
Value	$ 10,000

Although this approach might be useful to establish a very wide price range to screen out candidates that are obviously too large or small for the buyer's budget, it is viewed by most experts as a very misleading approach for establishing a more accurate level of price. The key criticism of the profitability method is that it fails to take into account the difference in value based on differences in cash flow and differences in capital expenditures required to generate earnings.[9] Two companies can actually have the identical sales and earnings but differ substantially in cash generated and capital expenditures required over time.

Value of Assets

A second approach to valuation and pricing is based on the assets of the company excluding its goodwill.

---

[9] T. Copeland, T.Koller, and J. Murrin, *Valuation: Measuring and Managing the Value of Companies*, New York: John Wiley and Sons, third edition, 2000. Chapters 3 and 4.

In early stages of negotiations, you are not likely to have direct access to information to make a determination of true market value of the assets. For this reason, a common pricing tool is to consider the net book value of assets. The *net book value* is the net sum of the depreciated assets, cash, receivables, buildings, equipment, minus the trade payables and accrued liabilities. Different industries may have different multiples, as with the profitability method. In the durable goods manufacturing companies that JP Industries Inc. and JPE Inc. investigated, for instance, a multiple of one or two is often used as a rule of thumb. If the asking price is much greater, say, three times book value of assets, it may be depleting its assets at a more rapid rate than depreciation schedules and would include a significant level of good will. In the event of a high multiple, therefore, you have to be sure the nature of the business is such that it can operate at that ratio without major investments. The book value of assets can be deceptive. Depreciation schedules often have little to do with the remaining market value of a particular item. Computers for instance, often depreciate more quickly in value than the accounting rules might suggest. On the other hand, real estate is regularly depreciated to zero dollars every ten years even though the property has plenty of retained value. Thus, an appropriate valuation of assets requires a direct evaluation of the inventory, equipment, facilities and other assets.

Raw materials are generally easy to value because such material can be purchased at a determined price. Work in process is much more difficult because such material cannot be sold until more work is done to it. Finished goods, once again are easier to value, especially if an established price has been set for the goods. Accounts receivables have to be examined closely. More aged receivables are worth less than those less than thirty days old. Older accounts receivables may be uncollectible.

Whether based on market value or net book value, the asset-based valuation approaches do not incorporate goodwill. The total value of the company is simply the sum of the net assets. Neither do these approaches take into account the time value of money. They do often provide a bottom-line figure of what the bank might be comfortable with but often generate figures too conservative for the seller to accept. It might be an appropriate method where the seller is losing money, and the assets have immediate value to the buyer, perhaps a company in the same industry interested in the inventory and equipment. However, as mentioned earlier, as a quick comparison to the valuation based on net earnings, as a way to identify potential problems in underutilization or overutilization of assets, this approach can provide some insights into the prospective deal.

Historical Cash Flow Approach

The *historical cash flow* approach is probably more similar to the profitability ratio method than to the discounted cash flow method. Using the historic cash flow method, pre-tax profit is adjusted upward, by adding back in the depreciation, bonuses and owner's draw, interest expense, and decrease in working capital. Pretax profit is adjusted downward subtracting for taxes paid, increase in working capital, and purchase of fixed assets. Using the historical cash flow approach, an average cash flow is calculated for a multiyear period. Then a multiple is applied, which is somewhat arbitrary, once again varying based on industry or other norms. Thus, for example, you might estimate that the average cash flow is $10,000 per year. In a particular industry, a multiple of five might be used:

Average cash flow/year:	$10,000
Multiple	x 5
Valuation	$50,000

The historical cash flow approach is an improvement over the net earnings approach because it reflects actual cash rather than paper profits. However, the historic cash flow approach still lacks a reflection of what is likely to occur in the future. And as with the other approaches based on a multiple, the accuracy of the valuation estimate is very approximate, at best.

Discounted Cash Flow Method

The discounted cash flow (DCF) approach to valuation is the only approach presented thus far which takes the time value of money into account. That is, it recognizes the fact that a dollar today is worth more than a dollar tomorrow. This is a very important concept in business valuation because you are basically giving the owner money today to gain the right to future cash generated by the business. To make a proper valuation, you should assess the value of the business relative to holding the money and investing it in some other way. The DCF approach also factors in a forecast of likely future performance of the company, assuming no changes or improvements by the buyer.

Two key concepts essential to calculation of value, according to the discounted cash flow method are *free cash flow* (FCF) and the *discount rate*. FCF is defined as the "after-tax operating earnings of the company plus non-cash charges less investments in working capital, property, plant and equipment, and other assets."[10] In the discounted cash flow model, future dollars are always considered to be worth less than present dollars. The discount rate refers to the percentage that dollars (or other currency) reduce in value on an annual basis. The factors that are often considered in calculating discount rate and the associated net present value include the opportunity cost to the buyer—that is, the return one could get for his or her money in other investments of the same risk, the tax benefit, and the after-tax cost. Deriving an accurate discount rate may be one of the most complicated but important aspects of applying this model.

Based on the DCF model, the total value of a company is equal to the sum of the present value of the company's free cash flow and the present value of after-tax nonoperating cash flow. You add up the earnings flow for the next five to seven years, first discounting the contribution from each year to the net present dollar value based on the discount rate that you determine to be most appropriate in your situation.

Free Cash Flow: An Example

Using the definition of DCF given previously, we can put together an example of estimating FCF for a hypothetical operation for a couple of years to demonstrate the components that must be considered in this type of calculation.

---

[10] Copeland, Tom, et al, *Valuation: Measuring and Managing the Value of Companies.*

FCF (in millions)	Year 1	Year 2	Year 3	Year 4	Year 5
Revenues	20.0	24.0	26.0	30.0	32.0
Operating Costs	18	21	22	25	26
Operating Profit (EBIT)	2	3	4	5	6
Taxes on EBIT	0.4	1.2	1.6	2.0	2.4
Operating Profit after Tax	1.6	1.8	2.4	3.0	3.6
Depreciation	.5	.6	.6.	.8	.9
Operating Cash Flow	2.1	2.4	3.0	3.8	4.5
Change in Working Capital	0.2	0.2	0.3	0.4	0.4
Cap Expenditures	0.5	0.5	0.6	0.7	0.7
Other Assets Invest	0.1	0.1	0.1	0.1	0.1
Total Investment	0.8	0.8	1.0	1.1	1.1
Operating F.C.F	1.3	1.6	2.0	2.7	3.4

The Average Discount Rate

The average discount rate and the resulting discounting factors can be estimated in accordance with the example below. Let us assume that the debt is 30% of total capital and therefore the equity is 70%. If the rate of opportunity is other investments is assured to be 10% for debt and 15% for equity, and the tax rate at the time is 40%, then we can calculate the average rate of discount as follows:

Capital	% of	Operating Rate	Tax Benefit	After Tax Cost	Portion of Rate
Debt	30	9.5	40%	5.7	1.7%
Equity	70	14.0	--	14.0	9.8%
AC of Cap					11.5%

The Value Beyond Forecasted Period

It will be very cumbersome to estimate the value of a company that one assumes to have a life for an indefinite period. A practical approach is to take a long-enough period after which the discount factor is miniscule and calculate the value for that period. A reasonable result is obtained by deciding the net after-tax profit by the average discount rate.

The Debt

The discounted value of the current debt should be estimated by using a rate that corresponds to the market rates of similar risks for debt. Future additional debts should not be included in the calculations since those debts would be balanced out by the repayments, appropriately discounted for that debt.

Equity

Finally, the equity value and correspondingly the value of the company is the sum total value from the operations for the forecasted period of ten years in this case and of that beyond the ten years minus the discounted value of the debt.

Let us look at an example of ***discounted free cash flow*** evaluation. Let us suppose we are looking at a prospective acquisition candidate for which its FCF for operations is calculated for ten years forward. The discount rate factor is also estimated for these ten years rising at an average discount rate of 11.5%.

Year	Forecasted: Free Cash Flow	Discount Factor at 11.5%	Present Value: Free Cash Flow
1	1.3	0.90	1.2
2	1.6	0.80	1.3
3	2.0	0.72	1.4
4	2.7	0.65	1.8

5	3.4	0.58	2.0
6	4.0	0.52	2.0
7	4.5	0.47	2.1
8	5.0	0.42	2.1
9	5.5	0.38	2.1
10	6.0	0.34	2.0
Value beyond 10 Yrs	58.0	0.34	20.0
DFCF from Operations			38.0
Debt			25.0
Equity			13.0

Which Technique to Use?

You may find it useful to use several of the valuation techniques presented in this chapter at different points in the negotiations process. The profitability and value of assets methods provides a quick assessment of the general value of the company early in the negotiations process and does not require much technical assistance. However, as you get closer to finalizing the price you wish to pay, you are advised to obtain the assistance of an appraiser experienced in the discounted cash flow approach to obtain a much more accurate valuation of the company.

Early in the process, the JPE team calculated the net book value of the assets of a prospective company and then compared it to the value of the company based on the profitability ratio using a P/E ratio of 5. Then the team made a judgment as to whether the relationship between assets and price makes sense. If the assets are much lower than the value based on the earnings, it looked more closely at the company's fixed assets to make sure that the equipment and facilities had been kept up-to-date and whether other necessary investments had been made to keep earnings at that particular level in the future. As mentioned before, owners of companies with low assets compared to price may have stopped investing in the future of the company.

The next step in the valuation process is to carry out the more detailed discounted cash flow analysis, looking at the next three to five years, based on current operational plans, *not* those necessarily that JPE Inc. planned to implement. This is important. You should never value a company based on how you think you can get it to perform after changes are made. The valuation should be based on what the owner is presently doing. In sum, our acquisition team used at least three of the valuation methods—net book assets, P/E ratio, and discounted cash flow methods—in succession as it got more involved with a company and was able to learn more about it. However, the discounted cash flow method is considered the most accurate of the three and the one upon which final value is most closely based.

Other Factors to Consider in Pricing a Company

Once you have developed a fairly rational assessment of the value of the company using the combination of methods described, you still need to arrive at a price that you feel is appropriate to pay for a particular company. There is no set formula for this because the worth of a company will vary depending upon the buyer. An important concept, especially where an existing company buys another company is the potential synergy of the acquired company with the buying company. Bill Pursche (1988) identifies three types of synergies, universal, endemic, and unique.[11]

Universal synergy Universal synergy is generally available to any acquirer with capable management and adequate resources. Examples of universal synergy might be an economy of scale or larger market share in an industry.

Endemic synergy By contrast, endemic synergy may be available to only a few acquirers, perhaps companies already in the same industry.

Unique synergy Finally, a unique synergy may be an opportunity that can be exploited *only* by a specific buyer (or seller).

---

[11]   Pursche, Bill, "Building Better Bids: Synergies and Acquisition Prices," Chief Financial Officer USA Magazine, 1988.

Although these categories are more typically applicable to existing companies purchasing others, individual buyers may vary in their skills and background and thus gain greater or less benefit from a particular purchase.

Some Differences in Valuation across Industries

The nature of assets is a key factor that affects the valuation procedures across industries. A manufacturer can more easily identify hard assets such as machinery, equipment, tools, receivables, inventory, and buildings. By contrast, the asset approaches are much more difficult to carry out and perhaps less relevant in service businesses where goodwill constitutes a large part of the company's value. Because the discounted cash flow method does not depend upon valuation of assets, it can be more universally applied. However, due to the lack of hard assets, banks may be more reluctant to finance purchase of service companies. Although this is a financing issue, it can also dampen the overall price.

Other valuation-related issues should be considered in the service industry. In a service business, you are basically buying intellectual property. It is much harder to test the value of intellectual property than in manufacturing, where you can see, touch, and feel property for quantity and quality. For the service company, you need to evaluate whether the services offered are state-of-the-art, if those services are needed in the market, if the services will sell, and if those services have a future. You also need to consider the uniqueness of the business. The company's uniqueness may stem from legal protection, such as a copyright or patent, or may stem from the unique capabilities of the technical or management people assembled or the long-term relationships built with customers.

Also consider compatibility when valuing a prospect. When Burroughs bought Sperry Rand, for instance, their software and design were not compatible, and they had a hard time rationalizing the two businesses. Eventually, the conglomerate shrank back to the size it had been before Burroughs acquired Sperry.

Cultural fit is another consideration for both service and manufacturing. If you have a culture surrounding one person, when that person leaves, the company may not have the same value. It is preferable to purchase a company with knowledge and leadership that is more widespread. You cannot force anyone to stay, even with an employment contract.

It is important to remember also that multiples vary by industry if you plan to use the profitability ratio or the historic cash flow methods. You need to find other comparable companies that have been bought or sold, which might be difficult in an industry that has few transactions.

Chapter Summary

This chapter introduces some of the basic concepts of valuation of the company. Although four basic approaches—the profitability method, the asset method, historical cash flow, and discounted cash flow are all described, the discounted cash flow method is considered the most accurate valuation of the company. However, a comparison of values from different methods can provide useful insights, especially in the early stages of valuation of the business.

This chapter also points out the distinction between value and price. The value is the worth of the company as will be operated by the buyer. The price is the amount you wish to pay for it. The synergy you can realize from the sale, the motivation of the seller, and the projected growth of the industry, and the type of financing are just a few of the factors you might consider in negotiating the final price.

Suggested Further Readings for Valuation

Merfeld, Eugene and Gary L. Schine, *How you can buy a business without overpaying*, New York: The Consultant Press, 1991, Chapter VII, Valuing the Business.

Copeland, Tom, Koller, Tim and Murrin, Jack, *Valuation: Measuring and Managing the Value of Companies*, New York: John Wiley and Sons, third edition, 2000, Chapters 3 and 4.

CHAPTER 12

NEGOTIATING THE DEAL

Successfully negotiating the deal requires a clear understanding of the negotiation process. This chapter presents a view of the negotiation process that will help you to be a more effective negotiator. Negotiation needs to be viewed as a problem-solving process. Your goal should be to establish a positive atmosphere of communication and trust. Such an approach is likely to increase the odds that you actually close the deal and develop a sound business relationship with the seller after closing. To be successful, you must be well-informed—about the company you plan to purchase and the industry. You should also understand a seller's motives for selling, but don't waste too much energy on fancy techniques designed to psyche out the seller. Further, you must avoid romanticizing or "falling in love" with any one deal. Being a good negotiator does not require fancy tricks, "bamboozling" or bluffing the other side or reading tiny signals of body language. It requires that you, as the buyer be as informed as possible about the situation—the seller's motives and details about his or her company and the industry. Finally, good negotiation also requires that you know exactly when you are going to walk away from the deal and when the seller is likely to do so. When you have that clarity, you can be a tough negotiator.

Negotiation begins with the first phone call to the broker or seller and continues through closing. Different aspects of negotiation are usually covered at different stages or steps in the acquisition process. This chapter also reviews some of the more common reasons that sellers sell. An understanding of the seller's motives is likely to assist you in structuring a deal successfully. This chapter closes with some other tips that will help you to be a more effective negotiator.

Negotiation: A Problem-Solving Process

Negotiation is a problem-solving process by which two parties converge on the same solution. In the acquisition process, the buyer and seller must concur on a variety of terms expressed in the purchase agreement that documents the sale. Looked at in this way, negotiation requires the identification of issues and problems that need to be resolved. The buyer and seller must work out acceptable solutions to these issues and problems. To accomplish this task, various arguments may be set forth, proposals made, and individuals persuaded until all parties involved in the sale arrive at an agreed point of view.

In short, in the final analysis, negotiation is a process that involves resolving business issues that result in financial payment to the seller in some form, whether it be cash, notes, or stock for buying the company's assets and operating activities.

Know the Company and Industry well

Successful negotiation depends, first and foremost, on thoroughly knowing and understanding the company and industry with which you are dealing. Accurately estimating value and foreseeing potential problems and opportunities require a thorough understanding of the company you are planning to acquire and the industry it operates in. If you lack direct work experience in this particular industry, you may need to do extra homework at the library and to talk with others in the industry.

Depending upon the industry you are investigating, information might be available through a trade association or other published resources at the library, such as Standard and Poor's Industry Survey, Predicast, Value Line Industry Reports, and online business publication databases, and other possible resources. Your local university or public library reference librarian should be informed about materials available to you.

It is remarkable how much printed material is available for most of the major industries.

If you are investigating a relatively new or small industry, you might find less available in print. However, trade associations often have valuable reports and publications even for relatively specialized industries. You may talk to typical customers if the company services other businesses or to manufacturers' representatives. Typically, previous work experience in a particular industry is also a very valuable way to learn who you can contact for more information.

Learn the Seller's Motives

To be a successful negotiator, you should also have a thorough understanding of the seller—his or her motives for selling and his or her fears about selling or the selling process. This is such an important area that we will explore this area in detail later in the chapter.

Maintain Control of Business Decisions

Don't let your consultants manage you or the negotiation process. Successful negotiation also requires the effective management of parties other than buyer and seller. Although attorneys are needed to work out many legal aspects of the purchase agreement, they should not serve as the negotiators for business-related issues that are not strictly legal in nature. Similarly, you must keep the accountant's role in proper perspective. Although various accounting details need to be resolved, in the end, the buyer and seller must develop a deal that is comfortable to them.

Establish a Positive Atmosphere with the Seller

It is important that you maintain an atmosphere of open communication and trust with the seller throughout the negotiation process. To assure that you reach a closing, it becomes essential that a positive atmosphere is developed in which the buyer and seller view negotiation as a process for finding solutions to issues and not as a means to create an adversarial atmosphere. Certain support people, especially attorneys, may need to be managed carefully because their involvement can often lead to a more adversarial atmosphere. On the other hand, it is probably better to be dealing with a well-versed, competent attorney than to be delayed indefinitely by a first-time seller who does not know what he is doing.

Build Rapport with the Seller

Successful negotiation and consummation of a sale often requires a certain chemistry between buyer and seller, especially if the company is privately owned. The typical seller may have spent many years building his or her company and may have ambivalent feelings toward its sale. He or she often has an attachment and obligation to long-time employees and may be reluctant to sell the company unless he or she feels it will be taken care of properly. The importance of comfort and trust between buyer and seller should not be underestimated.

Don't Try to "Psyche Out" or Bluff the Seller

Some treatments of negotiation devote too much attention to adversarial tactics such as bluffing or "psyching out" your opponent. Do not concentrate too heavily on this aspect of negotiation, or you will miss the main point of negotiation. It is helpful to know how the other side thinks, what the seller's priorities are, his or her concerns, and style of negotiating. Consider also whether or not he or she is prone to bluffing, is argumentative, or prefers a rationale based on facts and numbers. But the critical aspect of negotiation is that you want to keep the momentum of discussion moving to keep the process moving forward—not spending all your time determining an opponent's body language!

Narrow the Gap in How Buyer and Seller Perceive the Target Company

Much of the negotiation is really a matter of balancing the perceptions the buyer and seller each has of the value attached to different parts of the

---

business. Typically, the seller tends to pay more attention to the positive aspects of the business and may be less willing to accept the problems that a buyer might identify, especially those problems that may significantly devalue the worth of the company. Acknowledgment of such problems is necessary, however, to come to terms with adjustments to a finally agreed-upon price and terms.

Say for instance, that as a result of your preliminary due diligence, you offer ten million dollars in your letter of intent. But then during the formal due diligence process, you begin to uncover facts of which you were not previously aware. Perhaps you uncover a pollution problem requiring expensive cleanup or liabilities for a pension fund that had not been properly accrued. You have to convince the seller, first of all, that these problems exist, and that secondly, they should reduce the overall price of the company by $2 million. A good negotiator is able to persuade the seller that this point of view is valid and is able to convince the seller to accept the new price or at least some price in between the old and the new one. However, if there is a lack of trust between buyer and seller, this is much more difficult to accomplish. Some frequently negotiated topics relate to inventory value, pollution problems, and negotiation of other reserves.

Differences in perception in inventory value Inventory valuation is a common area that often requires renegotiation of price. A seller might perceive his inventory to be perfectly good, but when the buyer evaluates it, he or she might find that a part of the inventory only moves once in every three years or may be altogether obsolescent. There is no fixed formula to devalue slow-moving inventory. Thus, when inventory is a significant proportion of the total assets, it usually becomes an issue for negotiation.

Pollution problems: another negotiation topic The cost of environmental cleanup is another problem. The exact cost may not be precisely pinpointed in advance unless the seller agrees to take care of the problem before closing. But this is not always feasible, or the pollution problem might be a pending future threat (i.e., slow-moving groundwater that has been polluted by factory waste). Negotiation involves not only the agreement of a final price but also the amount of reserves that will be held in escrow for a period for these possible "future" liabilities.

Negotiation of other reserves Other reserves typically cover workers' compensation claims, bad receivables, and deferred taxes. In each case, the seller and buyer must agree on how much each issue or problem impacts the price or the amount of the reserve. The buyer or the seller are not necessarily trying to bluff or taking advantage of the other side. It is usually more a matter that each side has different perceptions of the situation. Perhaps the seller feels it is only necessary to put $2,000 in reserve. But you have done your own investigation and determined that $10,000 is a more appropriate reserve for a pollution problem. This is where the development of trust between buyer and seller can be quite helpful because you as the buyer must persuade the seller that you are not trying to squeeze him on price, but that the pollution cleanup will likely cost about $10,000. This is only one example of dozens of issues that might crop up prior to closing.

How to convince the seller to accept a variance to the agreed upon price Following the rational model laid out thus far, convincing the seller to accept a lower price or a higher reserve amount requires your accurate understanding of experience by other businesses in your industry. For instance, you need to research what reserves are typical in that type of business. You might obtain a balance sheet from another company and share it with the seller. Or you might share other knowledge obtained from work experience in the same industry.

If you do not know what your peers are doing, then you should be able to rely on your accountants or auditors, who will often know. Thus, if you reach an impasse with the seller, you might suggest that the two accountants get together to work things out. With proper guidance, the accounting firms can often come up with a good compromise. They will review the details and history of the company. For instance, if the dispute involves workers' compensation reserves, the accountants can review the seller's workers' compensation experience. They might note that a recent spike in costs is not typical of historical data and come back with a more likely scenario of future costs. However, you will need to understand what changed in the business to cause the recent increase. In a case of slow-moving inventory, you have to work with the seller to convince him or her that it is not your role as buyer to cover the seller's bad business calls (in a tactful manner, of course). Sometimes when you really reach an impasse, you may simply agree to split the difference or change the terms of the deal in some other manner, such as how much is paid in cash at the closing date.

Timing and the Negotiation Process

Unlike some of the other aspects of the purchasing process, such as preliminary or formal due diligence, negotiation begins with the first call to your broker and continues until closing. However, certain aspects of negotiation tend to take place at different times.

Negotiation and Price

Most of the price negotiation is typically done prior to signing the letter of intent. Although neither party is legally bound by the price agreed to in the letter of intent, it is advisable to be as accurate as possible, given the information available to you. Otherwise, you run the risk that the seller might change his or her mind about selling later on after you have spent more time and money during the formal due diligence period.

On the other hand, if information surfaces during the formal due diligence that has a major effect on your valuation of the target company, clearly you need to negotiate more acceptable price terms with the seller. Pollution cleanup costs, unreported liabilities for a pension fund, or pending lawsuits from a former employee or customer might affect the price. However, contingencies, such as a threatened lawsuit or possible cleanup are treated differently than costs that are known. These uncertainties may be handled differently in the contract by negotiating an escrow amount.

Using the Purchase Agreement to Surface Problems

Negotiation of the purchase agreement is an extremely helpful tool in surfacing problems you may not learn about otherwise. That is why we recommend that you begin work on the purchase agreement as early in the formal due diligence process as possible.

The purchase agreement is the first legally binding document in which the seller maintains that he or she has fairly and openly represented the company accurately. The consequence of hiding information is straightforward. The selling owner is bound to reimburse the buyer for costs that the buyer can prove were intentionally hidden, i.e., that the seller knew about but chose not to reveal. The buyer's attorney or other legal representative may point this out explicitly to the seller early in the development of the final purchase agreement. Surprisingly, this reminder frequently surfaces new and important information affecting the valuation and pricing of the company.

Negotiation of Escrow Amounts

In the course of investigating the target company, you may learn of potential problems that are not yet resolved, such as a threatened lawsuit or possible pollution problem. Rather than adjust the price, sellers and buyers may negotiate terms in the purchase agreement to set a certain amount of money in escrow for a set period until such an issue is resolved. This type of negotiation usually takes place after the letter of intent is signed as such issues surface during a more formal due diligence process.

Meeting with the Seller

An efficient acquisition search depends upon a clear understanding of your seller. You want to find out as early as possible in the acquisition process, first of all, whether or not you are dealing with a willing seller and secondly, whether or not the seller is a reasonable individual. Just as the seller expects you to be a credible buyer, you need to be concerned about whether or not the seller is credible. You don't want to waste your time with an individual who is not serious about selling or who is going to be unreasonable throughout the negotiation process.

Reasons for a Sale

It will help you in the negotiation process to understand why the seller is selling his or her company. He may not always come right out and tell you at first, and the initial reason given may not be the primary or accurate one. But if you are able to build rapport with the seller and spend enough time communicating with him or her, eventually you will figure out the true reasons.

A seller may have several legitimate reasons for selling a business. This section presents some of the more common reasons.

Settling the family estate In our experience, the most common one for a private owner is the need to settle a family estate. Based on current tax laws in the US for instance, capital gains are generally taxed at a much lower rate than an inherited estate.

A need to "smell the roses" Another commonly given reason is that the owner does not want to take risks any more. He or she wants to "smell the roses" so to speak. Interestingly, in our own experience, the most likely time that most people who sell for that reason, other than for an estate, are between fifty and sixty-five years of age. Over sixty-five, although of course there are exceptions, typically the owner does not sell. Either the estate issue is not relevant—perhaps the heirs are already well-taken care of—and/or the seller has reached the point where he or she hasn't developed any outside interests or hobbies. The company itself *is* the hobby so the owner doesn't sell. It is often much tougher to buy a company from a healthy seventy-five-year-old than from a fifty-year-old owner!

Overwhelming challenges An owner may also decide to sell when some change in the business or industry, which makes it difficult for the owner to continue to manage effectively. These changes may have left the company short of capital, too large to manage, or in a poor market position to compete given the company's current resources and available management skills. These are all legitimate reasons for selling. But depending upon your own skills and access to resources, you need to carefully evaluate your ability to take over such a company and run it successfully.

Lack of strategic fit Large, publicly held companies have other motivations to sell than does the private owner. Typically, the divestiture of a particular unit takes place because it does not fit strategically with the rest of the company, the parent company decides that the market is too small, or the division is not as profitable or growing as quickly as the parent company desires. Such divisions can also be a good opportunity, depending upon your own background and ability.

The owner is burned out You should be especially cautious of purchasing a company that is run by an owner who has lost the drive to compete. Such a company may have already fallen into such disarray from the standpoint of facilities upkeep, employee morale, or customer reputation that it may not be worth purchasing. Watch out for repeated comments by the owner about the competition. If your prospect is a manufacturer, you want to explore how recently the company has developed a new product.

Why You Should Learn about the Seller's Motives

You have several negotiating advantages if you can learn the seller's motives for selling.

Gauging whether the seller might back out of the deal First of all, the strength of the owner's motivation to sell will give you a guideline as to how hard you should push for concessions or compromise to your point of view. Especially among smaller companies not represented by an investment banker, the owner may be ambivalent toward the sale. It is not uncommon for a seller to cool toward the idea partway through the sale and change his or her mind. Even when the seller has signed a penalty clause in which you recoup formal due diligence expenses, you can never recoup the lost time that could have been spent on a sale that would have been consummated. If you learn that a seller is not very motivated, you may be well advised to drop the lead and consider a different prospect.

Gauging which compromises might be appealing or likely Secondly, the seller's motives may guide you in the types of compromises to

174

negotiate during the acquisition-negotiation process. For instance, if the sale is motivated by estate reasons, then you are likely to assume that tax considerations, especially tax savings, might be a valuable bargaining chip for the seller. Timing of the closing, for instance, might affect the year in which taxes are due. This may be more important to the seller than to you as the buyer.

Gauging the likelihood of serious problems Finally, the seller's motives might reflect knowledge about pending changes in the competitive structure of his or her industry. A large competitor might be moving into his or her territory. Or a major customer may have cancelled a long standing order. Although such issues should surface during due diligence, it is important to learn of serious problems threatening the business early on in negotiation so you can evaluate whether you are prepared to deal with them.

Don't Romanticize the Deal

One of the most important aspects of being a tough negotiator, i.e., of negotiating to your best advantage, is to know exactly when you would walk away from the deal. It also requires that you realize that you should be ready to walk away from *any* deal, regardless of how much money you might have sunk into it up to that point. Don't make a deal just because you have spent a lot of time and money on it unless the deal really makes sense. This phenomenon, the perceived need to pursue a course of action solely because of the time and effort already expended, is referred by management experts as *escalating commitment*. Even experienced managers fall into this trap from time to time.

In short, regardless of the money spent, if at a particular point it is clear that the purchase would be a mistake, or the price has simply become too expensive, you must remember that there are always alternatives out there. Critical to your negotiating strength is the maintenance of a lead flow throughout negotiation and clear thinking up to the closing of the deal. Don't stop looking once you have signed a letter of intent or even when you have completed formal due diligence.

Chapter Summary

Perhaps too much has been written about elaborate or indirect negotiating techniques in business situations. At least in the case of acquisitions, we espouse a direct, problem-solving-oriented approach. This builds trust between buyer and seller and allows for resolution of key issues.

Thorough understanding of the seller's motives and details about his or her company and industry will aid your negotiating ability. You should thoroughly understand the prospective company, including the likely risks and potential problems you might encounter if you take over ownership. Further, you should be able to present such concerns in a way that the seller will find believable and acceptable.

You may run into a seller whose perception of the company is too different from your own to resolve in negotiation or in some other way becomes unreasonable. For this reason, it is *always* critical that you keep your lead flow going. This may necessitate having a cash reserve or going back to investors for more money so that you can investigate other leads. Be cautious about holding all your "eggs" in one basket. Keeping your leads flowing will also reduce the chance that you romanticize any one deal. Also keep in mind that there are always other "fish in the sea." You want to guard against escalating commitment, the phenomenon that you become more strongly committed to the deal just because you have invested more time and money in it. No deal is perfect, but if you really uncover a major concern, it is never too late to back out of a deal prior to closing. It is better to lose $30,000 or even $100,000 than to pay $500,000 or more for a business that is headed for serious trouble.

RECOMMENDED READINGS FOR CHAPTER 12

1. "The rule of the four P's in Tuller, Lawrence, *Buying In: A complete guide to acquiring a business or professional practice*, Liberty Hall Press, 1990. pp107-111
    This short reading describes the four P's: People, planning, perception and patience.

---

2. "Why Sellers Sell" in *How you can buy a business without overpaying* by Merfeld, Eugene and Schine, Gary L, New York: The Consultant Press, 1991, pp.15-20.

    This reading goes into more detail about the reasons for selling, including retirement, the owner is bored or fed up with the business, the need for a regular paycheck, a good offer comes up, family-life changes, spouse job change, the business owner gets a job offer, future growth limited by management abilities, and need for investment capital.

3. "Seller Perspective versus Buyer perspective, in *How you can buy a business without overpaying* by Merfeld, Eugene and Schine, Gary L, New York: The Consultant Press, 1991,pp. 21-22.

    This reading describes in more detail the theme of the emotional attachment to the business by the small company owner, seller optimism, potential mistrust between buyer and seller, and the notion that some sellers think that no one else can run their business.

4. "Chapter 13: Negotiating the Purchase", in *How to buy a business* by Joseph, Richard, et al, Enterprise, Dearborn, 1993, pp. 198-208.

    This chapter has several suggestions for negotiating, including some common traps and suggested guidelines.

CHAPTER 13

FINANCING THE ACQUISITION

You should begin planning the financing of your acquisition at the very start of your search. This includes figuring out how much you are likely to need and where you will get it. You help to establish your credibility with brokers and potential sellers early in the search process by providing evidence that you have the funds to carry out the deal should it go through.

How big a company you search for as part of your initial search parameters is dictated in large part by the amount of funds you can access. Conversely, the nature of the deal may dictate the level of interest you can generate for financing. The two issues are interdependent. Of course, you will not have all the details or commitments worked out from investors or lenders until they can examine the actual company you plan to purchase. On the other hand, you cannot afford to wait until you are well into negotiations, only to find that you lack a means for financing a deal. Thus, similar to negotiations, the process of obtaining your financing is likely to unfold throughout the acquisition process.

Estimating Your Financial Needs

Early in your search process, you want to figure out how much you will need. The amount of money you need to purchase a business varies greatly by industry. In the manufacturing sector, the price usually translates into one or two times the net worth of the company. In distribution, the multiple could be around three. You can ask your brokers what ratios to expect in the industries you are considering. You should get an estimate of what you need before your search so that you know what your goal is.

Funds needed to make the deal Figure out the expenses you are likely to incur for the acquisition itself. As mentioned in earlier chapters, it is not unusual to spend between $50,000 and $100,000 or more, depending on size and complexity of the candidate company to close a deal, including the costs of preliminary and formal due diligence, legal fees for contractual negotiations, and so forth. If you have a management team who can work for free, obviously you can reduce the overall cost somewhat, but it would be wise to develop a financial plan that covers not only the funds needed to close the deal but the initial costs of the acquisition process itself.

Debt-to-equity ratio Once you know the total amount of funds you will need, you also need to consider the ratio of debt to equity that you feel comfortable with. Many highly leveraged deals took place in the 1980s for as high as a ten to one ratio of debt to equity. However, these are very risky endeavors, and many companies fell far short of succeeding in servicing this debt. Psarouthakis generally tries to limit the debt-equity ratio to three or less. In the manufacturing sector, this ratio provides a better cash flow cushion in a company-downsizing scenario in case the economy suddenly takes a nosedive.

To keep everything in balance—your assets, debt level, cash, inventory, payables, receivables—you need to be very cash-flow sensitive, not just accounting sensitive. A conservative debt-to-equity ratio will allow you to manage your assets and generate cash flow to respond to loan covenants. Thus, resist the temptation even if the banks are willing to go higher. Be very wary of a bank or other lender that encourages a highly leveraged position. They may be the ones owning your business at the next business downturn, not you! When you are too highly leveraged, even with careful management of your cash and inventory levels, you can run into serious problems servicing the debt.

Types of Funding Available

In addition to figuring out your funding needs, you should also figure out where you will get the funds to buy the target company. You may have to investigate a combination of several different sources and types of funding to cover the entire price of the deal. Funding generally falls into two overall categories: debt and equity.

Types of Debt

Before describing different sources of financing, we will review certain basic financing terms, including *secured* versus *unsecured debt*, *primary* versus *secondary debt*, *mezzanine debt* and *revolving credit* or *working-capital debt* (also referred to as an operating line) and *equity*. Let's review these terms briefly.

Secured versus unsecured debt Secured debt is a loan backed up or "secured" by some type of collateral, whether from the company to be acquired, your personal sources, or another company, if an existing company is doing the purchase. An unsecured loan is just that. There is no collateral to back up the loan in case of default.

Primary versus secondary debt In the case of limited funds, there is a pecking order established from the start as to who gets paid first. Typically, secured lenders are also in a primary position. In the case of liquidation, secondary position lenders are paid after primary lenders.

Mezzanine debt Mezzanine debt bridges the gap between loans from traditional-secured lenders and equity contributors. Equity kickers or other arrangements might be used to attract one of these lenders. The seller, for instance, may provide some of the mezzanine debt not covered by equity and other bank loans. Convertible bonds are a common form of mezzanine debt. Insurance and finance companies are also often interested in this type of debt. Mezzanine debt is senior to equity, usually junior to bank debt and often converts to equity over a period.

Revolving credit Revolving credit, also referred to as an operating line or working capital debt, is a short-term debt usually secured by accounts receivable, inventory, or both. It is always in a primary position against short-term assets.

Equity

Equity sources are funds contributed by owners in the business. In the event of a liquidation, proceeds are distributed to equity holders only after creditors are satisfied. On the other hand, whereas the return for debt is usually for some specified, fixed amount, equity holders are unlimited in potential returns, depending upon the earnings and asset growth of the business. Thus, this source of financing has both the highest risk and the highest reward.

Sources of Debt Financing

Within the general category of debt, you may choose among several types of lenders depending upon the availability of collateral and your business reputation. Some of the most common sources for secured and unsecured debt financing are discussed in this section, including commercial banks, finance companies, insurance companies, pension funds, and the seller.

Commercial banks Although first-time buyers are probably most familiar with commercial banks, they are an unlikely source of long-term debt financing unless they have a finance company subsidiary. However, they are a primary source of working capital or revolving-credit financing. In your initial planning stages for buying the business, therefore, it is worth establishing bank relations for your new business even if you don't use services from a commercial bank immediately.

If you are turned down by a commercial bank, one option worth exploring is the U.S. Small Business Administration (SBA) loan. The U.S. government does not actually lend the money, but it does guarantee a commercial bank's loan in case of default. The SBA loan still requires collateral although it will often accept personal collateral if you lack assets in the business. Since the laws and regulations change from time to time, it is worth checking with your local Small Business Development Center or local Chamber of Commerce to obtain the latest information. Beware the personal loan guarantee requirement of the SBA loan however. You are not only risking your current personal assets but future assets as well.

Finally, consider a bank for short-term debt, if you have receivables, inventory, or real estate available for collateral and if the loan amount is under $1 million.

Finance companies Another type of financial institution, referred to as the asset-based lender, is more apt to provide you with an acquisition loan if you have hard asset collateral such as real estate, equipment, or machinery. They are also often willing to leverage the deal with a much higher debt-to-equity ratio than would a commercial bank. However, be cautious. Such companies can also be in the position to force an auction to liquidate the company for late payments. Check out the company you are planning to borrow from thoroughly with several customers before signing a loan agreement.

Use an asset-based lender for long-term debt, where you have machinery, equipment or real estate as collateral, and if the amount of the loan is in excess of $1 million.

Factoring companies are expensive and risky. They have no problem liquidating the business. You should avoid factoring companies in any deal.

Insurance companies Insurance companies can be good sources for loans and are often more patient than finance companies. Very large insurance companies specializing in life insurance are worth looking into. You probably won't be able to approach them directly, but a good merger and acquisitions consultant may be able to help you make contacts.

Pension funds Pension funds are another source of debt. Once again, you will probably need a third party to help you approach one of these sources. They vary in how involved they want to be with the business. Again, it is worth checking with other borrowers to see what their experience has been.

———

The seller Finally, if you still have a gap between the seller's asking price and the financing you are able to obtain from debt and equity, the seller is frequently used as a source to make up the difference. For instance, you might provide a note secured by inventory. Typically, sellers will recognize a much higher value for inventory, as high as 75% or even 100% of its value, as security for the loan, whereas a bank typically may provide only about 50% of inventory value in a loan, if it is used as collateral. In this type of loan, the seller can be placed in the first position before the bank but for inventory only. This would reduce the amount a bank might lend, but since you get a larger percentage to borrow against inventory, you increase the total amount of debt available to you to purchase the company.

Sources of Equity

Just as with debt, several sources of equity are available to you. This section reviews the more common sources.

Personal investment You must weigh several factors in deciding how much of your own funds to invest. On the one hand, you may want to maintain personal control over your company. On the other hand, you need to evaluate how much of your own capital you want to risk. If you are young and have no one depending upon you for financial support, you are obviously in a better position to take risks than an older person with family obligations. However, you also want to consider that if the venture is so risky that others do not want to be a part of it, you may be foolish to put all of your own funds into the venture.

Investment from family and friends One of the most common sources of capital for entrepreneurs is funding from family and friends, whether as a loan, equity, or both. You need to consider this source carefully. First of all, if these relatives provide part of your own financial safety net, you want to be careful not to overextend their personal commitment to the total business either. You also want to be sure that a complete loss of equity will not jeopardize important personal relationships in your life. Approach family and friends as you would a stranger—with a formal business plan, an accurate portrayal of the risks involved and a clear proposal for how the investment will be returned to the investor. By treating friends and family in a businesslike manner, you reduce the chances of misunderstandings that might jeopardize your friendship in the future.

Venture capital firms Increasingly, venture capital firms today manage funds for wealthy investors. Although discussed frequently, venture capital is a source of funds for a very small percentage of entrepreneurs. Venture capitalists expect a very high rate of return. If you plan to purchase a rapid growth, high-potential company, it may be worth investigating this avenue. Venture capitalists also look very closely at the experience of the management. They will be more interested in someone with previous entrepreneurial experience. However, many venture capitalists today prefer acquisitions to start-up companies, with the former being viewed as lower risk. It is worth checking into, especially if you are in need of large sums (half million dollars or more per venture capital firm).

Small Business Investment Companies (SBIC) SBICs are venture capital companies licensed by the federal government. The program began in 1958 as a way to make money available for small company investment. SBICs actually can provide either debt, equity, or both.

Angels and other private investors Angels are a much more common source of equity than venture capital firms. Angels are likely to be wealthy individuals interested in investing their own funds in an entrepreneurial venture. Area doctors, dentists, and successful businesspeople may be angels. Business opportunities are often screened for such individuals by lawyers, accountants, brokers, and business associates in the area. You may contact your network of business associates. Venture capital clubs in the larger business communities also often attract angels and/or their representatives. That is why you often see so many attorneys and accountants at such meetings, listening for good opportunities to recommend to their clients. As with a venture capital firm, you will need to prepare a detailed business plan to present at such events or to share with these contacts.

Investment banks Investment banks are a rapidly growing source of both debt and equity. Investment bankers increasingly serve roles other than that of the intermediary in the purchase of the target company. For instance, many also assist in putting together a financing package for an acquisition. For instance, it may pull in funds from other sources such as an operating line from a commercial bank or long-term secured debt from a financial institution. The investment bank might also provide some of the mezzanine financing and/or equity itself. Investment banks should not be confused with venture capital firms however. The latter is rarely interested in a debt position. Nor are venture capital firms likely to provide financial consultation. Try to find the right-sized investment banker for your size of firm. Although investment banks are not interested in very small firms, they are becoming a growing resource of funds and expertise for many entrepreneurs.[12]

Earn-outs and seller-employment fees Earn-outs and seller-employment fees are some other techniques used to close the gap between the agreed-upon sales price and the available debt and equity. An earn-out is an agreement whereby part of the seller's compensation for the business is based on the performance of the business after the deal is closed. It may be based on a percentage of gross sales, net sales, or net profits.

Consultation and employment fees may also make up some of the gap in the difference between other financing and the purchase price. In this case, the seller is paid a salary or consultation fee for his or her assistance in the transition of ownership. If you use such a fee, you should review current tax implications carefully with a tax consultant.

Sometimes the mere *timing* of the deal might affect the net cash to the seller—for instance whether the sale is closed at the beginning or end of a tax year.

Dealing with the Banks

Since most deals include a bank loan for at least a portion of the overall financing, it is worth examining some issues related to bankers' relationships in greater detail.

---

[12] A New Source of Money: Financing Through Investment Banks, in Tuller, Lawrence, *Buying In: A complete guide to acquiring a business or professional practice, Chapter 12*, Liberty Hall Press, pp. 175-186.

Shop around to different banks First of all, in spite of the ratios and numbers, you will find a wide variation in ratios across banks, whether it be debt to equity, earnings-to-interest ratio or some other yardstick. It is worth shopping around at different banks to see what they expect.

Minimize your personal risk Secondly, although it is a common practice to do so, we feel it is a mistake to use your house as collateral in a business loan. A bank asks for your house as collateral when they do not feel you have enough equity. The banks should say this directly, but they do not always do so. Rather than put yourself and/or your family at greater financial risk, you should seek other sources of equity to balance the debt. Decide on your limit and then inform the bank that this is all the money you are going to put in. If this approach doesn't work, you should consider searching for another bank.

Limit the bank's involvement in the business Third, some banks try to get too heavily involved in the operating aspects of the business. Ask the bank what requirements they have with respect to performance and outcomes, but don't allow them to get involved with issues that pertain to the management of operations. Management at JPE Inc. at times had to say point-blank to a banker, "Look friends, you know how to manage a bank. Just do that. We know how to manage operations, and we will take care of that. Tell us what covenants you don't want us to violate or what your requirements are in terms of performance so that you feel comfortable giving us the loan."

Be sensitive to the banker's needs Fourth, try to realize that sometimes the individual loan officer might be faced with internal issues that affect his or her behavior toward you. For instance, Tuller (1990) shares an anecdote about a loan applicant for a business that waited two months impatiently for a banker's answer. Annoyed, he almost walked away from the deal.[13] Tuller, who is an experienced business broker, contacted the banker to learn that the banker was concerned about meeting his quota for the coming month and was trying to push more business into that month. Tuller patched things up between the banker and his client. The client got his loan, and the banker was happy too.

---

[13]   Tuller, Lawrence, op cit

Beware banks with liberal policies Fifth, be cautious about banks and other lending sources that are too liberal in their policies, for instance in the debt-to-equity ratio. Sometimes a poorly run bank will call in their *good* loans before their bad ones because they need the money. Or they may be less understanding if and when you miss a payment. Check out your banker thoroughly to be sure that you feel comfortable with the type of business relationship that you will experience.

Financing when You Have an Existing Company

Most of the guidelines described so far pertain whether you are a first-time buyer or own a preexisting company. However, there are differences. In providing a loan to an existing company, a lender will examine the impact that the target company will have on the balance sheet of the existing company. You may be able to secure some of the debt with collateral from your existing company. And of course, you may have some cash or other assets available to invest in the target company from the existing company. Finally, you may have a longer track record and thus have an easier time obtaining a loan from the bank although commercial banks may still be wary of providing a loan for the direct purpose of purchasing a new company. However, the other sources of debt and equity and most of the other general remarks are still applicable, even for those who already own a business.

Chapter Summary

Financing the acquisition requires thorough and careful planning. You need to consider the different sources of funding accessible to you. The amount required for purchasing the company may dictate the types of sources that you seek out. Some combination of debt and equity is likely. Be wary of overextending yourself with too much debt. On the other hand, be careful to protect your immediate family by not taking too great a risk with your personal assets. It should not be necessary to put your entire life's savings up for collateral. If the deal makes sound business sense, but nevertheless, a bank or other lending institution starts making unreasonable demands, check out another bank, review your business plan, or try some other approach. Lending institutions vary from the unscrupulous to the impeccably correct. You need to be especially cautious with any lender that is likely to take your company away from you if you fall behind on a few payments. Check out your sources, both equity and debt, as thoroughly as you check out the seller. Are you dealing with honest individuals? Have you reviewed the fine print for hidden commitments that might jeopardize your ownership? The earlier you begin to develop your financing plan, the more likely you will be ready to close when the purchase agreement is finally negotiated and signed.

CHAPTER 14

PREPARING AN ACQUISITION
ACTION PLAN

Creating an acquisition action plan is one of the most important steps you can take to guarantee the success of the acquisition. Most companies probably do not bother with an acquisition plan. Of course, you will hear of the person who buys a company during a dinner meeting with a lawyer. But those are often the same people who are pulling their hair out nine months or a year later, wondering why they aren't making the numbers that they thought they would.

What is the Acquisition Action Plan?

The *acquisition action plan* is quite simply a description of what you plan to do once you take over ownership of your new company. Ideally, you should begin preparation of the acquisition action plan during the formal due diligence phase. That way, you have a plan completed and ready to put into operation the moment closing takes place. To prepare a good plan, first of all, you need to understand that company thoroughly, not just the industry that it operates in. Second, you need to determine whether the way the business currently operates is up-to-date and progressive or whether it needs to be changed. If you locate areas of poor performance, you need to identify specifically what causes the low performance so that you can develop an action plan to correct it.

Your overall action plan for change might include a series of shorter action steps in different areas of the company. Once you determine which changes are necessary, then for each change you should specify not only what should be done, but also *how long* it will take, *how much* it will cost, and *who* is going to do it. Also very important are your anticipated *results*. Since an action plan is implemented as a corrective measure, you should have a very clear idea as to the specific changes that should occur as a result of implementation as well as the financial performance changes, e.g., the amount of increased sales, profits, or other financial improvement you expect.

Objectives and Content of an Acquisition Action Plan

A good acquisition action plan has two objectives. First, it documents the results of the due diligence activities. Thus, much of the acquisition plan is a report that follows the structure of the due diligence. As or more importantly, however, it presents the recommended strategies and action plans to make that company into a successful acquisition. The acquisition plan must include who is going to run the company and what is to be done with it.

An acquisition action plan might include the following major sections, a preface, brief history and overview of the acquired company, an overview of the industry, a description of operations and organization of the newly acquired company, strategies and action plans to implement those strategies, and financial statements.

The *preface* to the acquisition plan may explain its purpose, especially if the report is to be shared within your management team. It might also include some other introductory material, such as the task force members involved in creating the document and a summary of the game plan as well as target dates for completion and who is responsible for each assignment. In the case of one acquisition at JPI, the following major phases were identified:

Phase 1: Assessment of current operations
Phase 2: Development of strategy and action plans
Phase 3: Finalize and sign purchase agreements
Phase 4: JPI assumes control
Review and document first-day actions:
  employee meetings
  customer notification
  vendor notification
  physical inventory calculation
  fixed asset appraisal
Phase 5: Post-acquisition implementation of action plans and follow-up

Brief history and overview of the acquired company This section of the acquisition plan includes a company description, history of ownership, reason for the seller's divestiture, product descriptions, financial summary, and key people.

Overview of the industry and market An overview of the industry includes an overview of the entire industry as well as market segments and the immediate competition. It details the existing and new products and customer information.

Company operations and organization Although the structure of this section might vary depending upon the industry, it is basically a thorough description of the current company operations and organization. For a manufacturing company, typical sections might include sales and marketing, manufacturing, distribution and warehousing, inventory control and purchasing, human resources, management information systems, service, and legal issues.

Strategies and action plans Though a shorter section than the previous one, this section may be the most important. It outlines the issues and action plans for all the major areas of the company. Ideally, one-page action plans are created that briefly outline an issue—a description of the current problem and perhaps a brief history relating to how that problem arose. Then, for each issue, a description is provided of the action to be taken and the person responsible for taking that action. Ideally also, you should include a brief estimate of the budget, the time line in which that action should take place, and the expected results, if applicable, in financial performance terms.

In the case of a manufacturing company, plans might relate to general or administrative issues, including management succession plans, as well as marketing and sales, manufacturing, warehouse and purchasing, human resource, legal, environmental, and safety issues. Although it is helpful to consider issues by department or functional issue, do not neglect other issues, which might cut across departments or areas, such as the resource allocation system, work flow between departments, corporate culture and employee relations, overall quality issues, and the relationship of the company to the broader community.

Financial statements The acquisition plan also should include the historical financial information as well as forecasts and projections. Historical financial schedules should include the income statement, balance sheet, cash flow and accounting policies. Projections should include these same areas. It can also include assumptions and a narrative of the growth plans for the acquired company.

The Acquisition Action Plan and the Company's Value

Whether you are paying above or below book value, an acquisition action plan is essential to help guarantee the future value of the company. The presence of an action plan does not provide an absolute guarantee of success. However, in our view, the lack of an action plan greatly increases the risk of failure of the new acquisition.

Especially if you buy a company that is performing well, you are likely to pay a price that includes a goodwill payment in addition to the book value of the company. What this really means is that you are paying for the company's expected future performance. Thus, a certain level of growth in sales and earnings needs to be achieved once you take over in order to justify the price and the return that you get.

On the other hand, if you buy a company that is below book value, you have probably done so because the company is currently not operating at its full potential. However, it is just as critical that you identify specifically the areas in need of immediate attention, or you may find that your "bargain" company is worth even less after you take over ownership.

Leadership in Developing the Acquisition action Plan

Appropriate leadership in the development of the acquisition action plan is critical to its success. In the case of a very small company acquisition, the new owner is likely to be involved in both the development and implementation of the plan. However, in a larger company, it is not unusual, though ill-advised, to have one set of executives involved with the acquisition process up to the point of closing. Then the company is handed off to a second set of executives to run the company once it is purchased. This may be one of the major reasons why many acquisitions have a poor performance record. The acquired companies are not necessarily bad companies, but an appropriate takeover plan may be lacking.

Even if an action plan is developed by the acquisition team, if it is turned over to someone else to run, that new person doesn't own the plan psychologically, intellectually, or otherwise. Quite likely, the person taking over midstream will reject the action plan drawn up by others and start all over again. The transition from the acquisition team to a long-term team of executives occurs well after the closing date. In the case of a turnaround, new management is brought in prior to closing to carry out due diligence, develop the acquisition plan and implement the plan after the closing. In companies that are already performing well, existing management may be involved in each of these phases, together with management from corporate headquarters. In either case, the executives involved with the evaluation of the acquisition are the same ones who lead the development and implementation of the acquisition plan after closing. This way, management develops a feeling of ownership and responsibility for the acquisition.

In the case of one company purchased, the owner/manager told us from the beginning that he did not plan to stay on to run the company once it was purchased. Before proceeding too far into the negotiations process, we needed to decide who was going to run the new division. We found a former colleague for the position and brought him in to develop the acquisition action plan and to run the new division.

Sometimes you may buy a company where the former owner would like to stay active with the company. This happens more frequently when the owner does not own the whole company. This can present its own challenge because it is not unlikely that a year or two after the closing, he or she begins to cool to the idea of staying on. You need to decide what to do during that period. Should you hire a new person as an understudy? Do you place the owner in an advisory role? These are issues you need to work out in the action plan as well so that you are prepared later on.

Even if your company is relatively small, if you plan a second or third acquisition over time, it is very important to have the managers who will run the new division actively involved prior to closing with the evaluation of the company so that they can develop an appropriate acquisition action plan.

Involvement of Employees in Developing the Acquisition Action Plan

Starting in the formal due diligence phase or at whatever phase you are first allowed to meet with and talk to employees, you are likely to find them a rich source of information about improvements and changes already under way and/or those being considered. Development of action plans should not only involve the top leadership but also employees at the lower or middle levels of the organization. For instance, perhaps they are already aware of management information system problems and have been investigating a new system. You want to find out what they have looked at and why they have considered or rejected various plans. This would appear to be common sense, and yet, not all companies take the time or value the input from this source because they have not taken the time to plan.

Chapter Summary

You can easily get so caught up in the acquisition process itself that you delay proper planning of the takeover until after closing takes place. This would be a big mistake. Successfully executed acquisitions require months of planning prior to closing to assure a smooth transition. Much of the preliminary work overlaps with a properly done formal due diligence—extensive evaluation of the company and identification of potential problems. The remaining work, some of which may be obvious and some of which might require more problem-solving creativity, involves identifying the necessary changes and improvements that should take place and an assignment of due dates, budgets, and people responsible for carrying out these changes. A simple format is to create a short one-page action plan for each topic identifying the issue, the action required, who is responsible, and when it will occur, along with a budget and expected results.

The acquisition action plan may be the single most important thing you can do to assure the success of your new company. It is viewed as an extremely critical component of the successful acquisitions. The chief (principal) operating person must be involved in the process from the start.

CHAPTER 15

CLOSING THE DEAL

This chapter reviews the key elements of the purchase agreement. Once you have found the right company, lined up your financing, completed due diligence, and agreed upon a price, you are ready to close the deal.

The Purchase Agreement as a Due Diligence Acquisition Tool

Although you don't sign the purchase agreement until due diligence is complete, you should begin work on the purchase agreement at the same time that you begin formal due diligence. This is very important.

First of all, negotiations may take some time, and there is no reason for additional delay. More importantly, as mentioned in the chapter on formal due diligence, the negotiation of the purchase agreement document itself might surface problems that the owner forgot about, overlooked, or purposely hid during the course of due diligence. It is desirable to learn of these problems as early as possible in the negotiations and due diligence process so that further investigation of them will not delay closing, and in the worst case, that you have minimized your expenses on due diligence if you decide to walk out of the deal altogether.

The warranties and representations section of the purchase agreement holds the owner liable after the close of the deal for expenses or charges that he or she could have foreseen and did not warn you about. However, from a practical standpoint, you should always assume that it may be difficult, if not impossible to collect damages once the deal is closed. Therefore, the key purpose of the representations and warranties section is to learn about major problems during the due diligence period and address them in the purchase agreement. Unsettled lawsuits or other threatened liabilities can then be addressed with appropriate amounts of money held in escrow for a reasonable period based on the specific contingency being protected against.

Elements of the Purchase Agreement

The four basic sections of the purchase agreement include the following:

1. Price and terms of the sale
2. Representations and warranties
3. Conditions and covenants
4. General statements of law.

In an *asset purchase agreement*, assets are transferred from the seller to the buyer in the sales transaction. This is often the case when a larger corporation divests itself of a particular division. In a *stock purchase agreement*, the purchaser may acquire stock ownership in the company rather than assets. Because of the lack of hard assets, a stock purchase agreement is the most common form in service companies although it can occur in other types of industries as well.

The actual purchase agreement for a medium-sized corporation may be quite lengthy, with about 20-50 pages of narrative in the core document, not counting all the attachments, which may involve other agreements, such as the escrow agreement. The total agreement is quite lengthy. Exhibit 14.1 shows a table of contents for a stock purchase agreement. Exhibit 14.2 shows a table of contents for an asset purchase agreement.

Price and terms and conditions of the sale Terms of the purchase agreement cover the sales price, and the amount of cash, stock and assets that will change hands and any earn-out agreements. This section also describes what is being purchased.

Representations and warranties This section may elaborate further in describing certain aspects of the business, such as financial statements, benefit plans, patents, etc. More importantly, it is a statement of guarantee by the seller that everything he or she has told the buyer is true and that he or she has told the buyer everything of significance about the company to be purchased. How strong the guarantee itself is worded is often a heavily negotiated area. Disagreement over this section has caused deals to fall apart. However, it is vital that some language be included to protect the buyer that the company has been fairly and accurately represented.

Conditions and covenants This section lists all those items that must be completed by both buyer and seller prior to the close. For instance, in an asset sale, the seller must comply with the state's Bulk Sales Act. Or if the buyer wants to continue with the same insurance policies, the seller promises to deliver such policies prior to closing. Another example is the transfer of a real estate or equipment lease. This section is fairly straightforward, and a good attorney should be able to help you with all the necessary aspects.

General statements of law Other technical issues relating to state laws, arbitration procedures, and other legal issues need to be included with which a good contract lawyer should be familiar.

Types of Set Asides and the Escrow Agreement

Set asides are specified sums of money put into an escrow account by the seller at closing to be transferred to the buyer under certain conditions described in the purchase agreement or related escrow agreements. Two common types of set asides include inventory escrow and escrow for potential liabilities.

Inventory Escrow

Some money, often between 20-50% of the value of inventory, is held in escrow for about 30-60 days until an audit is finished, to verify that

---

the dollar amount of inventory promised is indeed in the warehouse and is saleable. There may be set asides for other price adjustments based on the results of the final audit. Sometimes an alternative approach is to sign the purchase agreement and then delay the actual closing for a period of thirty days or so to complete the final audit and then transfer ownership on the day of closing. Either way, you want to be sure to have a final audit to verify that everything that is included in the contract is physically present. Inventory moves in and out the door every day so you need an accurate audit as to the value when you actually transfer ownership.

Escrow for Potential Liabilities

A second type of set aside is included in an escrow for potential liabilities. You would be wise as a buyer to negotiate this second set aside as well. Usually an agreed upon percentage of the total price, possibly as high as 10% may be kept in escrow for up to twenty-four months or more to cover potential liabilities, such as employee or product-related lawsuits or other unforeseen liabilities that can be traced to problems occurring prior to the sale. Especially in medium-sized to larger companies, news media attention seems to bring various lawsuits out of the woodwork that had been dormant for a period. The twenty-four month time span is useful because it is typically during this time that media attention triggers interest by people who believe that this is their golden opportunity to sue the company. Transfer of ownership also may attract the attention of government bureaucrats. In the United States, you might catch the attention of the U.S. Environmental Protection Agency (EPA), the Occupational Safety and Health administration (OSHA), the Equal Employment Opportunity Commission (EEOC) or any of a number of other agencies that monitor business activities.

The set aside carries interest in favor of the seller and if nothing comes up within the designated time, the buyer releases the money to the seller in addition to agreed-upon interest. The escrow agreement clarifies what these funds should cover. You are wise to cover possible liabilities in this way than to assume that you can collect from the seller after the closing. Without sufficient escrow, you can try to pursue the seller through the courts, but collection can be a serious problem in all but the largest corporations and can be extremely difficult from a private seller. In addition, you incur the added time and expense of investigating the situation and taking it through the courts.

Legally, *disclosure* is the key in determining whether or not the seller is obligated to pay the purchaser for liabilities created prior to the transfer of ownership. Disclosure laws do not require that the seller discuss problems openly with the purchaser. Provision of related documentation, even if buried in thousands of other documents is usually considered sufficient.

Consider the following example. Say, for instance, a former employee who worked for the previous owner sues and wins a $2-million settlement. Perhaps you had information that the employee was disgruntled, which surfaced during due diligence procedures and requested $1 million be held in escrow. Because the seller disclosed the problem to you, and you agreed to the $1 million amount, he or she does not owe you the difference. On the other hand, in company B, suppose that the seller, for whatever reason, *had not* revealed a problem to you about this one employee. Then, you are entitled to the extra million dollars. On the face of it, it may seem better to allow such problems to remain hidden. However, consider that it may be very difficult to collect such funds. To reiterate, you are wise to investigate any letters, suits, warnings, or other signs of disgruntled employees or customers prior to closing rather than to attempt to collect from the seller after the fact. Such information will then be used to establish an appropriately sized escrow account.

The Closing Dynamic

Aside from the preparation of the legal documents, the closing may have two affective aspects worth understanding—the fear of closing and the closing momentum.

The fear of closing Especially within privately owned companies, the seller may have ambivalent feelings toward the sale. If the business has been in the family for a long time, or the seller is coupling the sale with retirement, a variety of emotions may come into play. On the other hand, when you deal with corporate sellers, such as the division of a larger corporation, you are not likely to experience this dynamic.

Closing momentum Ideally, you want the momentum of the acquisition process to keep moving forward through closing so that negotiation does not stall out. As the private seller nears closing, business ambivalence may give way to the excitement and momentum that builds as they begin to plan for their transition after the sale. The seller is more personally involved with the consequences of the sale going through or not than in the case when you are dealing with the corporate sale. Thus, whereas you are less likely to encounter a fear of closing among corporate sellers, you may run into a greater likelihood of the process slowing down or losing momentum as closing approaches.

Chapter Summary

This chapter reviews the closing of the deal. The key aspect of this step is the preparation and signing of the purchase agreement and other documents needed for closing.

Beyond the legal requirements of having a purchase agreement, the preparation of the document itself is an important aspect of the due diligence process. Because of the representations and warranties a seller is obligated to vouch for, frequently, problems surface during this period that you may not otherwise uncover. For this reason, it is very important to begin work on the purchase agreement as soon as the letter of intent is signed and you begin formal due diligence.

The momentum of closing and emotions attached to it may vary substantially, depending upon the type of seller with which you are dealing. With a divesture from a large corporation, you are less likely to deal with a fear of closing. The company has strategic reasons for spinning off the particular division you are buying. On the other hand, you may not have the closing momentum and urgency that builds when dealing with the private seller.

In addition to working out details of the purchase agreement during the due diligence process, you should concurrently work on the action plan for the days and weeks after closing. Chapter 14 already covered some of the key points to consider in developing such an action plan.

RECOMMENDED READINGS FOR CHAPTER 15

From Tuller, Lawrence, *Buying In*, Liberty Hall Press, pp. 198-204.

Exhibit 15.1. A sample of a table of contents for a stock purchase agreement

1. Definitions ....

2. The Merger..........
   2.1. The Transaction..........
   2.2. Adjustment to the Purchase Price..........
   2.3. The Closing..........
   2.4. Deliveries at the Closing..........

3. Representations and Warranties Concerning the Transaction..........
   3.1. Representations and Warranties of the Company..........
   3.2. Representations and Warranties of the Buyer..........

4. Representations and Warranties Concerning the Company..........
   4.1. Organization, Qualification, and Corporate Power..........
   4.2. Capitalization..........
   4.3. Consents..........
   4.4. Brokers' Fees..........
   4.5. Title to Assets; Sufficiency..........
   4.6. Subsidiaries..........
   4.7. Financial Statements..........
   4.8. Events Subsequent to Most Recent Fiscal Year-End..........
   4.9. Undisclosed Liabilities..........
   4.10. Legal Compliance..........
   4.11. Tax Matters..........
   4.12. Real Property..........
   4.13. Intellectual Property..........
   4.14. Inventory..........
   4.15. Contracts..........
   4.16. Notes and Accounts Receivable..........
   4.17. Powers of Attorney..........
   4.18. Insurance..........
   4.19. Litigation..........
   4.20. Product Warranty..........
   4.21. Product Liability..........

Exhibit 15.2. A sample of a table of contents for an asset purchase agreement

6. Purchase and Sale of Assets ....
   6.1. Purchase of Assets ....
   6.2. Excluded Assets ....
   6.3. Transfer of Assets ....
   6.4. Nonassignable Items ....

7. Related Agreements ....
   7.1. Assumed Liabilities ....
   7.2. Excluded Liabilities ....

8. Closing ....

9. Purchase Price ....
   9.1. Initial Adjustment ....
   9.2. Payment ....
   9.3. Final Adjustment ....
   9.4. Allocation of Purchase Price ....

10. Representations and Warranties of Seller ....
    10.1. Organization ....
    10.2. Power and Authority ....
    10.3. Approvals and Contents ....
    10.4. Title to and Condition of the Assets ....
    10.5. Real Property ....
    10.6. Leases ....
    10.7. Proprietary Rights ....
    10.8. Litigation ....
    10.9. Contracts; Agreements ....
    10.10. Employees ....
    10.11. Financial Statements ....
    10.12. Absence of Changes or Events ....
    10.13. Undisclosed Liabilities ....
    10.14. Environmental Matters ....
    10.15. Licenses and Permits ....
    10.16. Employee Benefits ....

Exhibits

Exhibit 1	Bill of Sale
Exhibit 2	Assumption Agreement
Exhibit 3	Balance Sheet of Seller at _____, 200-___
Exhibit 4.1	Adjusted Purchase Price
Exhibit 4.2	Secured Promissory Note
Exhibit 7.1	Assignment of Proprietary Rights
Exhibit 7.2	Supply Agreement
Exhibit 8.4	Escrow Agreement

Schedules

Schedule 1.1	Fixed Assets
Schedule 1.2	Assigned Agreements
Schedule 1.3	Real Property
Schedule 1.4	Prepaid Expenses and Account Receivable
Schedule 1.5	Excluded Assets
Schedule 2.1	Excluded Liabilities—Healthcare Coverage Schedule
Schedule 4.4	Allocation of Purchase Price
Schedule 5.3	Approvals and Consents
Schedule 5.4	Condition of Assets and Tooling
Schedule 5.6	Leased Real Property
Schedule 5.7	Proprietary Rights
Schedule 5.8	Litigation
Schedule 5.10	Employees
Schedule 5.11	Financial Statements
Schedule 5.15	Permits
Schedule 5.16	Multiemployer Plans
Schedule 5.17	Benefit Plans
Schedule 5.18	Insurance
Schedule 5.19	Related Third Party Transactions
Schedule 5.20	Recalls
Schedule 6.3	Approvals and Consents

CHAPTER 16

AFTER THE DEAL IS CLOSED: SMOOTHING THE TRANSITION TO NEW OWNERSHIP

This chapter describes some of the key steps you should take within the first days and months after closing. Once you have closed the deal, you must do certain things immediately, even the morning immediately following the closing. This chapter will give you some general guidelines that you can use to plan your own actions during this critical period and why we think these guidelines are important to follow. The suggestions provided are intended as general guidelines that apply to most types of businesses.

Objectives of the Transition

Within the first days and weeks after you take ownership of a new company, you have a window of opportunity within which to accomplish the following key objectives:

a. To build trust and confidence in you as the new owner by your key constituencies: your employees (management and nonmanagement), customers, suppliers, and the investment community.

---

b. To review and revise the company action plan developed during the due diligence period, now that you have actually taken over ownership of the company

c. To take steps toward making the major changes implied by your action plan.

The actions you take, even on the first day after closing, set the tone and the likelihood of accomplishing these objectives in a satisfactory way.

The First Day after Closing: Meetings to be Set Up

In our experience, the following order of meetings should be organized for the first day after closing takes place:

a. An initial get-together with management
b. An all-employee meeting
c. A more formal business meeting with management, which takes place after the all-employee meeting

These meetings lay the groundwork for accomplishing the objectives of the transition to new ownership. There are two reasons for making sure these meetings take place the first day and in the specified order. First, word gets around fast that the new owner has arrived, and everybody gets fidgety and nervous. They are asking themselves who the new owner is, what he or she is going to do, and so forth. Gossip and rumors start to circulate. The longer you take to introduce yourself, the longer such disruption takes place and the longer potential misinformation circulates.

Second, by holding the all-employee meeting before the more formal business meeting with management, you will get a good indication prior to the management meeting of the mood or overall climate among employees. For instance, is it stressful or blasé? Is there a level of high or low trust? Are people generally supportive or suspicious? Employees are not good at hiding their feelings. Their words and nonverbal behaviors can reveal a lot if you pay close attention to them. If you obtain this feedback from employees (both management and nonmanagement) before your first formal meeting with management, then you can discuss your concerns at the management meeting. In short, you need to put the human factor first.

Note that even though you hold these three meetings the first day, you will probably hold several additional meetings over the next several days. But you should do everything in your power to have these initial meetings on the first day so that no time is wasted before you begin to sit down with your employees to introduce yourself to them, to answer questions to put certain rumors to rest, and to build trust. In that way, you can more effectively start working on the content aspects of the transition.

The Initial Get-together with Management

On the first day, you actually want to meet with the management twice, once informally, prior to the all-employee meeting, and again later, in a more extended business-planning meeting. You hold the first meeting to accomplish three things:

1. To introduce yourself formally and to provide the opportunity to be properly introduced, in turn, to your management staff—their names, titles, and responsibilities.
2. To arrange for an all-employee meeting so that you can talk to all employees (to include everyone—both management and nonmanagement)
3. To provide a conceptual idea of the agenda for meetings to come in the first few days—especially, your intentions to review the action plan together with management.

The All-Employee Meeting

The all-employee meeting should be scheduled as quickly as possible on the first day after the initial get-together with management has taken place. Prior to the start of the meeting, you need to circulate around and get a sense of what the employees are thinking and what the overall atmosphere is like. Are people tense and worried or relaxed? This will help you in gearing your words and tone toward the group in an appropriate manner. Once the meeting begins, the following should take place:

a. You will formally introduce yourself as the new owner to all employees.
b. You should share with employees why you bought the company and what you believe you can or should do with the company.
c. You should explain to all employees that there is an action plan but that management must review the plan more thoroughly now that the ownership transition has taken place.
d. Finally, be sure to open the meeting to questions and respond honestly and responsibly to them.

Hopefully, being included in the meeting will help give all employees the feeling that they have been brought on board.

Note that unless you are very clear about it, some managers may reinterpret an all-employee meeting to mean only hourly workers and not management or other staff. The importance of including everyone from a team-building aspect should be obvious, but it is important to stress at the initial management meeting that you insist that everyone in the company attend. One time, when a meeting was called for a JPI acquisition, the manager brought in only the hourly workers. John Psarouthakis, one of the authors, asked, "What did you do with the rest of them? Did you fire them?" The manager answered, "Oh, you meant, *all* employees." "Yes," Psarouthakis answered, "I meant *all* employees."

The Formal Business Meeting with Management

After the all-employee meeting, you are ready to hold the first formal business meeting with management. The following three agenda items need to be addressed:

a. In more thorough terms than in the initial meeting, the need to review the action plan
b. The opportunity for each manager to share issues, concerns, or priorities at the top of his or her list

c. Discussion of a plan to address the constituencies outside the firm, especially customers and suppliers.

Review of the action plan If you have followed the advice of previous chapters, as a new owner, you already have developed an action plan prior to closing of the deal. However, since the plan was developed prior to the transition to new ownership, you cannot be sure that the plan reflects the most appropriate course of action or was based on the most accurate picture of your new company. Commonly, at least some of the employees, customers and/or suppliers may have been a bit suspicious of your motives during the due diligence period and thus may have been on their guard when providing their input. After all, at that time, these people did not know whether or not you were going to be the new owner—you and your representatives were total strangers. They may not have lied to you necessarily, but they may well have communicated less openly to you than they would to an actual owner. And of course, certain aspects may have changed in the meantime. Now that you have taken over ownership, therefore, one of the very first things you must do is to determine whether and in what aspects the action plan needs to be updated.

Though it is a good idea to mention briefly the need to review the action plan at both the initial management meeting and at the all-employee meeting, at the first formal business meeting, you begin to approach the review process in more detail. You should distribute copies of the action plan at this meeting, explaining at the same time that the plan was developed in the process of evaluating the company before the new ownership took over, and thus aspects may have since changed. You might want managers to look especially at those aspects affecting their areas and set a mutually acceptable date by which you will have a follow-up discussion of the action plan. You may need to give certain managers a few weeks to gather necessary information from customers, suppliers, or others to clarify some aspects of the plan. Keep in mind this is probably the first time most if not all the managers have seen the action plan in its entirety, even if they might have provided input previously into the plan. Thus, it is not productive and even problematic to discuss it until everyone has become more familiar with it.

Primary issues faced by management It is important to ask managers at this meeting what they consider to be primary issues of concern that need to be addressed immediately. Perhaps the prior owners were procrastinating on some key issue. At this point, you want to be careful to serve primarily as a listener after opening up the discussion. You should hear their views one at a time, encouraging a give-and-take atmosphere rather than individual monologues by you or your managers. You also want to be sure to give every manager the opportunity to express his or her views about the issues with which she or he is dealing, how urgent these issues are, and how long they have been a concern. In short, you want to see what management believes are the issues the new owners should address. These may or may not be the most critical issues from your perspective, but you want to give them the opportunity to relate their thoughts to you. Concerns may come from several sides—employees, customers, suppliers, product mix, equipment problems, or other production issues, such as training or retooling needs.

It is important to set the tone of an open climate for discussion. Managers should feel that any issues may be raised—whether they are rumors about layoffs or competitive aspects that are important to that manager, but due diligence didn't reveal. You can structure more specific discussions at later meetings, but this part of the meeting should be as open as possible to any topic that management might want to raise.

Finalizing a plan to address outside constituencies Finally, at this first formal meeting with management, you want to develop the basic outline of a plan to address the customers, suppliers, and other outside constituencies such as bankers or other members of the investment community. For instance, someone from the company should be assigned to contact key customers and suppliers to inform them of the identity and philosophy of the new owners. It is helpful to share the overall strategy of the new owners, especially as it might impact these customers or suppliers. For instance, will the same parts be purchased from suppliers, or will there be a different type of supplier needed? Will the same products be available to customers, or will be there be shifts affecting availability of your product?

Depending upon how far you can get with this first meeting, you may not be able to list specific dates for every activity. But at least you

---

can lay out the landscape for the general activities to take place in the coming weeks and months, and preferably, who will be responsible for seeing them through. Once you have the big picture from this meeting, then you can work out a weekly, monthly, and even a quarterly schedule to take care of these changes until you have completed the transition of ownership. Expect this transition to take about nine months, on average, for routines to set in with the new ownership. Modus operandi is then established. Even if pursued diligently, this period of transition can range between six and eighteen months depending on the size and complexity of the company.

Addressing Concerns of Your Key Constituencies and Building Their Trust and Confidence

In taking over ownership of an existing company, you need to address the concerns of various constituents. This section describes some of those concerns in more detail. Four constituency groups require immediate attention when new ownership takes over: employees, suppliers, customers, and the investment community, especially the banks.

An Overview of the Four Constituency Groups

The *employees* need to know who the new owners are, what their intentions are, why they bought the company, and what they plan to do with it. Employees are usually most concerned with changes affecting job security and long-term prospects of job advancement. Will there be staff reductions or a major shift in strategy? What is going to happen now that the new owner has taken over? This is such an important area that we will discuss the concerns of this constituency group in greater detail.

The *suppliers* want to know who the new owners are. Will the prior relationships continue, or will there be changes? If suppliers are critical to your business, you should have a high-level person (yourself or a key manager) contact your key suppliers to communicate this information firsthand.

The *customers* are an extremely important constituency, of course. With a transition to new ownership, existing customers may be uncertain about whether or not they will continue to have a reliable supply of the product and/or services from your company. This uncertainty may even cause them to change suppliers. Thus it is important to address this concern early on. If your business relies on a small number of key customers, such as is the case for many manufacturers, it is especially important that you or one of your key managers contact each of these customers firsthand, to answer any questions they might have. When retail or consumer-oriented services businesses change ownership, they often develop a plan to communicate the meaning and implication of the transition, with a combination of general advertising to the community and perhaps direct communications to their customer list.

The *banks*—both those set up by the previous ownership as well as those involved with you prior to closing, want to know as soon as possible whether the guidelines on which they based their loans are still in place or have changed—for better or worse. They will be especially interested in changes you may need to make in the action plan now that you have taken over ownership.

It is very important that all the constituencies are contacted about the change of ownership and any major changes in company direction within two to four weeks after new ownership takes over. If your company is underperforming, then your constituents are probably already aware of that fact making it all the more important to let them know quickly of your plans for turning the company. Even if your company is doing well, constituents need to be informed if you plan to make changes to the product line or other services that you offer.

Special Concerns of Nonmanagement Employees and Management

Employees are perhaps one of the most delicate constituency groups to address in the changeover to new ownership. A clear understanding and appropriate response to employee concerns is critical for effective transition to new ownership. A new owner sensitive to these concerns is less likely to be viewed as an intruder. In particular, the typical

217

nonmanagement employee is likely to have one or more of the following concerns:

1. *Job Security.* Quite simply, most employees want to know whether or not they will still have a job under the new owner. After all, in the end, they didn't choose to work for your company because of the prior owner's blue eyes or because of your tennis game. They are there because they need employment, and the environment is positive enough that they have decided to get their income there in exchange for working for the company on a regular basis.

2. *Income Level.* Employees also want to know whether or not they are going to suffer a loss of income due to the change in ownership or will have to work harder to make the same money. This is likely to be a much greater concern in companies where employees are already aware that the company is experiencing financial difficulties.

3. *Location Stability.* Employees may want to know of any plans by the new ownership to relocate some or all of the business. These concerns, again, are likely to be heightened if employees are aware that the company is experiencing financial difficulties. Location may also be of greater concern if headquarters of the new owner is in another city.

Management personnel are likely to have these same concerns. In addition, they are likely to be concerned about company structure changes, which might impact not only their job security and income level but also their responsibilities and opportunities for advancement. Furthermore, management employees may be especially concerned about long-term growth prospects of the company since it can also impact their opportunities for advancement. Of course, hourly employees will also feel that their job is more secure and that they are more likely to get a raise if the company grows.

Before you address employees at the all-employee meeting, you will find it useful to get a sense of these concerns at your new company. The earlier you get a sense of them and the earlier you address them in a way that is constructive, the better. These concerns won't disappear and the stress associated with ambiguity related to the future of each employee can be extremely counterproductive.

Setting the Proper Tone with Employees

Content aside, the tone you set the first day will carry for a long time into the new business. It is important that you leave an impression after the first day that you're serious and you're not in a hurry where employees are concerned. Don't just say, "hello," "good-bye," and then leave them hanging. You want your employees to know that you are very interested in working together with them for the future good of their company, that you will do whatever it takes to make the company a success, and that you mean well. You also want to leave the impression that you're a "no-nonsense" type of person who won't waste time getting needed changes under way.

It is also important to come across as sensitive to others' responses. The first day, at the various meetings, you need to listen carefully to the points of view presented, even if you don't agree with them or they are stated in a hostile manner. Employees are usually under a tremendous amount of stress and uncertainty, and all don't share the same diplomatic skills that you might desire, especially under those circumstances. This provides a great opportunity to communicate your sincerity about being concerned about the future of the company, even if employee reductions may be required. Thus, it is important to be honest. For example, don't allay fears about layoffs on the first day and then announce that very program two weeks later. However, if you are forthright about the need for the employee reduction or some other major change and follow the plans as stated, the remaining employees will have more confidence about their future. In sum, from the start, be sure that you say what you mean, and don't make arbitrary decisions.

The Cost of Owner Inexperience

Inappropriate handling of employees on the first day can be remembered years later as one former wine importer recalls:

—In one of my early acquisitions, following the advice of my accountant, I stayed away much of the first day. The accountant had felt that the news needed to sink in that the company was being taken over. This turned out to be faulty advice. I stopped by finally at the end of the day to introduce myself. Everyone appeared friendly and open at the time, but in retrospect, I completely misread the situation. I was full of excitement about my new company and didn't sense the employees' apprehensions. Further, I made the mistake of misreading their willingness to stay after normal work hours to chat. Of course, I asked if they minded staying awhile to talk, and they expressed a willingness to stay, but I realized later this was only said out of fear of my position of power as the new owner. Even months later, when they finally told me my mistake and after I had apologized for keeping them late, they still felt I had so overstepped my bounds with them that first day that for years after, employees in that company regarded me with suspicion and thought I was insensitive to their needs. On that first day, they had thought their world might be collapsing at that moment, and I had unwittingly ignored this. Perhaps it would not have made a difference, but I felt that the transition could have been smoother had I spent more time with them early on that first day and discussed their concerns. In short, in twenty minutes, I lost a tremendous amount of goodwill that was never regained.

As with most employees of newly acquired firms, these employees were fearful of their job security and future with the company. The wine importer became much wiser (and more successful) in his later acquisitions, addressing employee concerns early on the first day of ownership.

Steps toward Making the Major Changes Implied by Your Action Plan

Dramatic changes need to be announced immediately because that is when employees expect them. But if you don't make these changes early on, then as time passes, employees begin to assume that there won't be any, their attitude changes, and then when you try to implement change at that point, it becomes very difficult and builds distrust.

Another reason for making changes early is that their implementation may require multiple action steps, which take significant amounts of time, and it is important to get started as soon as possible. For instance, if you plan significant changes in production technology, this in turn, is likely to involve employee training. The sooner you start planning the production technology change, the sooner management can start planning the type of planning needed, who goes to the training, when it will take place, and so forth.

How to Approach Employee Reduction

Employee reduction is such a common consequence of new ownership that it deserves special attention. Generally people are intelligent and not that naïve. If a company is underperforming, the employees are often the first to know it, even before the owners. They often desire changes since in the long run this tends to make their jobs more secure (if they can weather the effects of employee reduction, of course). They often realize that some level of employee reduction is essential to the long-term survival of the company.

Suppose you are faced with having to make employee reductions. There is no way to "soft land" this type of action completely, but you can do certain things to make it more acceptable. It doesn't help to blame people for being stupid or incompetent (especially not those you must continue to work with!). But it may well be true that the prior leadership or management (ideally, you want to avoid being too hard on current management) made decisions that had negative consequences. If so, you might need to explain that the prior ownership allowed certain activities to take place obviously intended well but with negative results that now need to be corrected. For example, a classic strategy error in manufacturing is the decision to continue making a certain product when it is clear that the product is no longer relevant to the market. Perhaps the previous ownership did not pay close enough attention to market changes or had emotional reasons that made it difficult to let go of the outmoded product. When this occurs, the corollary to that is that you often have more employees at all levels continuing to make that product contributing to overhead and a more unprofitable result. This unfortunately then triggers the need for employee reductions unless you can shift those employees to other product lines that are growing more rapidly. However, this is not always feasible. If not, it is important to share this picture so that employees understand why the layoffs must occur.

You must also have a specific plan for the layoff, not just walk in one morning and announce that 30% of the employees will be let go. Unfortunately, that is frequently what happens. If you are buying an underperforming company, in all likelihood, if you have carried out due diligence properly, you know you will face employee layoffs ahead of time. Thus, you can build in the employee reduction aspect into your action plan and the costs associated with its implementation. The programs you may want to provide laid-off employees should thus not only be part of the action plan but also part of the negotiations. If you do this, then you can be confident that you can afford the programs that you propose. For instance, if you feel it is appropriate to include placement help and retraining programs for employees that must be let go, you can factor these costs into the original price you pay for the company. You might negotiate a contract with local training centers and community colleges to update their skills. It is important to have a cap, in terms of the amount of time people have to apply for such benefits and how much money you are able to spend. For instance, you might have a 45-day limit for applying for such benefits and a certain number of days or courses of training that employees may take.

Environmental Issues

Remedying environmental problems are similar to employee reduction in that if you have done your due diligence thoroughly, you will know in advance that you will have to take some actions to remedy pollution or other types of waste problems. If you factor this into your action plan and subsequently into your negotiations, then you shouldn't have to deliberate further once you take over ownership whether you can afford to comply with the law. It is already built into your agreement. For instance with one acquisition, JPI had a problem with lead pollution at one of its plants. The previous and new owners negotiated a cleanup fund of about $5 million to be paid by the previous owner to cover the costs of cleanup. The agreement included the understanding that if less were spent, the balance would be returned to the former owners. On the other hand, if the cleanup cost more, JPI would have to cover the difference. In fact, the cleanup cost only about $4 million and the balance was thus returned to the former owner. This arrangement benefited not only the community but also employee relations since many of Jigs employees lived in the same community and appreciated the environmental responsiveness on the part of the new owners.

How to Get a Sense of the Place and Stay in Touch

During the transition period of six to eighteen months, it is important to remain involved with your new acquisition. It takes several months to complete the transition to new ownership. If you are not involved on a day-to-day basis as an owner-manager, it is important, nevertheless, either for you or in the case of a very large corporation, a designated representative to visit the company frequently. You can't expect to go in like a bulldozer for just a couple of weeks and then manage the operation long-distance after that. You need to be on-site to see how things are going, to sense how well changes are taking place, and to keep tabs on the climate or atmosphere. Using telephone, fax, or other contact, or bringing management from the new acquisition to the home office does not substitute for on-site contact with all levels of employees. Many new owners do not like to do this. Most people feel that if they visit the new company a few times the first month that this is enough. But this tends to be a mistake.

One of the challenges faced by the owner is how to carry out these visits, however, without undermining management. This task may be made all the more difficult if you are off-site much of the time, attending

---

to other aspects of the business or other companies that you own. You may easily find yourself undermining the authority of your management team if you are not careful. You have to be conscious of the fact that as the owner, your words have considerable weight, and your intent can easily be misinterpreted.

The goal of your visits should be to absorb information, not to tell people what to do. You should walk around the company, interacting not just with management but with nonsupervisory personnel as well. However, you need to be very careful not to undermine the existing management structure as you do so. It is tempting to issue direct orders when you see that something may need to be changed. But it is important to follow the chain of command—sharing your observations with the appropriate manager and allowing him or her to decide whether or not action needs to be taken, based on your input.

You also need to be careful not to override the chain of command, even unintentionally. This can happen quite easily if you are not careful as one of the authors discovered after a visit to one of his first acquisitions. As he was walking around one plant, he asked an employee why a piece of equipment was located in a certain spot rather than somewhere else. The employee gave a suitable explanation, to which the owner responded "fine, thank you," but nothing else. Nevertheless, on the next visit, the new owner discovered to his surprise that the equipment had been moved to the new spot. This change created two problems (a) the machine was moved to a less desirable location than where it had been before and (b) the employee's manager didn't know that it was being changed until he saw the piece already moved to its new location, and no doubt felt that his authority had been undermined. That's not very healthy. In sum, it is so easy for employees to misinterpret the questions of a new owner as a mandate. Thus, as you ask questions, it is helpful that you immediately follow the question by letting the employee know that you don't want actions taken based on your conversation—you are just trying to learn how things are done.

At times of course, you may uncover problems that require attention. If so, then you should go to the manager first and say, in effect, "While I was walking around, this was my impression, and I'm thinking that perhaps things need to change." If the manager agrees, then he or she needs to make the change, not you. Otherwise, if you go around making changes yourself directly then you render the management team ineffective. Even long-term owners make this mistake, but it is especially easy to fall into this trap as a new owner.

It can be very tempting at times to break this rule. But keep in mind that you may not have all the information even if the answer seems obvious, and that if you feel that immediate action needs to be taken, you should talk to the appropriate manager first. Consider this example: imagine that in your "walk" around the company, you discover from an accounts receivables employee that Customer A consistently pays in sixty days instead of in thirty days, in direct violation of general policy. It is tempting to interfere, perhaps suggesting that the employee needs to contact Customer A to get him back on track. If you react this way, of course, the employee will likely obey your orders. But perhaps Customer A has worked out a special payment plan with the department head. Perhaps the customer has only recently fallen into arrears or perhaps it is a very large client who has negotiated special terms. Therefore, if you forget to talk to the department head first, you have overridden his decision without knowing it. Thus instead of taking action, you should tell the employee, "Gee, that is too bad, but don't do anything until your boss or department head is consulted about it." It is for his boss to tell him what to do, not you. Of course, don't forget about the problem. If you think it is an important issue, you might go to the department head directly and ask why Customer A is paying in sixty days instead of thirty. Then listen to the manager's views and give him the opportunity to take corrective action instead of doing it yourself. You have to put your ego on the hold, from that perspective. Otherwise, your management will eventually become afraid to act when you are not there, and you will no longer be able to delegate effectively.

The lack of awareness of how an owner undermines his or her team is not unique to new owners. But particularly in the case of new ownership, employees are prone to take every word you say as an instruction of what to do, so you need to be on special alert.

Chapter Summary

Once you close the deal, you need to be prepared to go in the very next morning to meet with your management team as well as your entire staff. What you do in the first days and weeks will set the tone for your relationship with your employees for some time to come, possibly even the duration of your ownership. Remember that the chief concerns of your employees and managers may be somewhat different than your own agenda. Employees will be concerned, first and foremost, about their own job security and future with the company now that it is under new ownership. Management shares this concern and may also have more narrow issues facing them in their own departments that nevertheless they may feel requires immediate attention. An easy model to follow includes a short initial introductory meeting with management, an all-employee meeting to include all management and nonmanagement staff, and then a third more formal meeting with management. These meetings will set in motion the planning to carry out the three objectives of the transition: addressing your key constituencies (employees, customers, suppliers and bankers), revision of the action plan, and implementation of significant changes outlined in the plan. Other meetings will follow in the first days and weeks, but it is essential to try to fit these first three meetings into the first day if it is at all possible.

As a new owner, you must be careful to listen carefully, building trust and goodwill with your new employees. Although difficult to accomplish, even negative changes such as employee layoffs can be carried out effectively if you communicate your objectives clearly, follow through relatively swiftly during the early period of transition, and remain sensitive to special needs of employees going through such a transition. Layoffs in particular need to be carefully addressed since it also affects the morale of remaining employees. It is wise to anticipate the costs of major changes such as retraining and outplacement services for employee reduction or toxic waste cleanup for environmental issues in the original action plan and in the negotiated price for the company so that you can afford to carry out these actions in the early weeks and months.

One of the easiest mistakes to make as a new owner is to override the existing management structure. You need to be very visible in the early months, making contacts at all levels, not just top management so that you can spot problems and build rapport with your staff. At the same time, if you identify problems you feel are in need of change, you should strive to work within the chain of command. Rather than act unilaterally, go to the appropriate manager or direct an employee to do so. Otherwise, you will eventually make your management team ineffectual.

Most important of all, be patient. The transition may take a year or more. However, with proper advance planning, your reward is that you will increase the odds that you will realize the gains that you had anticipated when purchasing the business.

INDEX